HELGE SEIDELIN JACOBSEN

An Outline History
of Denmark

HØST & SØN

© *Helge Seidelin Jacobsen og*
Høst & Søns Forlag, Copenhagen 1986.
Fourth printing 1993.
Photos: Helge Seidelin Jacobsen.
Cover photo: Inga Aistrup.
Cover: Peter Lind.
Typesetting: N. Christensen Grafik ApS
Printed by Narayana Press, Gylling 1993.
Printed in Denmark 1993

ISBN 87-14-28664-5

FRONTISPIECE: Oldest representation
of Christ in Scandinavia, c. 965 A.D.
Detail from the big Runic stone of
Jelling, E. Jutland (p. 14).

Contents

FOREWORD

However small it is today, Denmark has a long and rich history, and is considered the oldest kingdom in Europe. It forms a bridgehead between the European mainland and the Scandinavian peninsula and thus guards the entrance to the Baltic Sea. This strategic location has been Denmark's weakness and strength at the same time. Large territories have been lost to our neighbours, but as a result of mutual jealousy among stronger powers Denmark has survived as a nation with its own language and culture.

My aim in this book has been to write a history of my country, following the chronology of events rather strictly and paying special attention to the international background and Denmark's relations with other countries. Another aspect has been to incorporate the mention of still existing historical monuments.

Although Denmark was one of the cradles of the study of non-classical prehistory – the terms "Stone, Bronze and Iron Age" were invented by a Dane – I have chosen only to give a summary of the more than 10,000 years of prehistory of the country. For this subject I refer to "Prehistoric Denmark", an illustrated booklet, published by the National Museum, Copenhagen, in 1978.

I have written the book in English, which is not, of course, my native language. I would like to thank my friend, Chris Lawson, a British journalist based in Copenhagen, for his help with the language revision of the manuscript.

Also I would like to thank two American friends, Dorothy Madsen Swanson of St. Paul, Minn., and David Hoerlein of Seattle, Wash., for their valuable suggestions.

H. Seidelin Jacobsen
Copenhagen, April, 1986

PREFATORY NOTES

I. The Geography of Denmark

Denmark is a Scandinavian country in Northern Europe at about 56° N and 11° East. It covers an area of 16,000 sq. miles (43,000 sq. km) and has a population of a little over five million. It consists of the peninsula of *Jutland*, which makes up ⅔ of the total area, and some 500 islands, of which 70 are inhabited.

Copenhagen, the Danish capital, is situated on the biggest of the islands, *Zealand*. Jutland and Zealand have each over two million inhabitants. The second biggest island is *Funen*. Between these provinces you find the three waterways to the Baltic Sea, i.e. *the Little Belt, the Great Belt* and *the Sound*, the latter between Zealand and *Scania*, which until 1658 was a Danish province, but since then a part of Sweden.

The surface of Denmark is a moraine formation, made up of glacial deposits from Scandinavia and the Baltic regions. Northern and Western Jutland is rather sandy and less densely populated than Eastern Jutland and the islands, which are more fertile. The subsoil consists of various kinds of clay, limestone and flint.

Quite different, however, is the island of *Bornholm* in the Baltic Sea (between Sweden and Poland). This is a rocky island of granite from the world's oldest formation (part of the Scandinavian range of fold-mountains), and only thinly covered by moraine.

II. Danish Names and Spelling

As to Danish place names the English versions are used whenever available, e.g. Copenhagen and Elsinore instead of København and Helsingør, etc.

As to personal names only long-established English versions are applied, e.g. in the case of such Viking kings as "Sweyn the Forkbeard" and "Canute the Great". Though it might seem natural to write "Margaret I" and not "Margrethe I", this might easily lead to confusion as the English equivalent of "King Hans" would be "King John". For this reason the Danish names have been preserved with the above mentioned exceptions.

At the end of the Danish alphabet, one finds three vowels unknown in English: æ, ø and å.

Æ (ae) is pronounced somewhat like the vowel of such English words as "egg" and "air". It corresponds to German and Swedish ä, and is preserved in the "British Encyclopædia".

Ø (oe) is very difficult to reproduce in English. The closest English equivalent is the vowel of such words as "hurt" and "blur". It corresponds to German and Swedish ö and French eu.

Å (aa) is a deep a, somewhat like a in "all" and "awe". In this book the old spelling with aa is used, e.g. in such place names as Aalborg (Ålborg) and Aarhus (Århus).

Prehistory

c. 12 000 B.C. – c. 750 A.D.

The Early Stone Age (c. 12,000 – 4,200 B.C.)

After the thick ice-cap which had covered most of what is Denmark today
had melted down at around 12,000 B.C., the tundra landscape was invaded
by large mammals such as bears and reindeer. Soon Man followed in their
footsteps. The animals were hunted down with clubs of bone or wood, reinforced with stone, and with spears or arrows with flint heads, but fishing
and food-gathering were important elements of life too.

After a new rise of temperature beginning c. 8,000 B.C. pine and birch
trees invaded the region, later to be followed by a great variety of decidu-
ous trees, primarily oak and lime (linden) and towards the close of this period also the beech. The woods provided shelter for deer, wild boars and
oxen. The melting ice of the Northern hemisphere caused the seas to rise,
and Denmark was split up into the peninsula of Jutland and the islands.

Refuse-heaps, called "kitchen-middens", from c. 5,000 B.C. reflect a rich
variety of oysters, fishes, birds as well as seals and other mammals consumed by man. Very recent excavations of the oldest burial place so far
found in Northern Europe, at Vedbæk, north of Copenhagen, from the
same time, give us an idea of a more advanced society than formerly sup-
posed. In itself an extensive burial place indicates that nomadic life had
been replaced by more permanent settlements, and the careful burials, e.g.
of a man resting his head on deer antlers and a small boy placed on a swan's
wing add a human and religious touch. The only domesticated animal in
the Early Stone Age was the hunting dog.

However late Denmark became inhabited, the Early Stone Age covers
a period of about 6,000 years, which in length of time equals all later peri-
ods, prehistoric as well as historic.

The Late Stone Age (c. 4,200 – 1,800 B.C.)

The difference between the Early and Late Stone Age is organized farming which appeared in Denmark c. 4,200 B.C. The knowledge of how to plant seeds, of harvesting and stock-keeping had been on a long, slow journey to Northern Europe from warmer regions.

People began to make clearings in the forests with flint axes and to construct houses of wood. Cereals became the main source of nourishment, and very beautiful pottery is characteristic of the period c. 4,000 – 3,000 B.C. The domestic animals were the ox, the sheep and the goat as well as shepherd dogs. Somewhat later the pig was domesticated.

The cultivation of land favoured social stratification reflected in the many stone cromlechs (or dolmens – see picture opposite page 16) from c. 3,500 B.C., the oldest preserved burial mounds, which must have been tombs of chieftains and places of worship. However, the somewhat later, very impressive "passage graves", i.e. burial chambers constructed of large granite boulders, may contain up to a hundred bodies, buried over a length of time. But whether these were for everybody or preserved for an exclusive number is still an open question.

What happened around 3,000 B.C is even more dubious. Perhaps a new people invaded and conquered the country with small horses and better weapons, such as the battle axe. Anyhow great changes of life took place. The art of pottery decayed, while great labour was invested in the perfection of flint tools and weapons, first of all exquisite daggers, shaped as if they were cast in metal as rare specimens of bronze had begun to find their way from more developed civilizations to the south.

In the Late Stone Age it is estimated that the population of the present Danish area rose from about 5,000 to 40,000 people, but such figures are of course highly theoretic.

The Bronze Age (c. 1,800 – 500 B.C.)

Because of its relatively low melting point, bronze, an alloy of copper and tin, was the first metal here and elsewhere to substitute stone in tools and weapons, but due to its scarcity it never replaced stone completely.

The valuable raw materials of copper and tin were imported from distant places, perhaps in Central Europe, but exceedingly fine objects were cast in Denmark, such as the big musical horns, called "lurs", of which a dozen are still playable after 3,000 years in the bogs, probably the oldest wind instruments in the world that can play.

In this apparently peaceful period it is likely that a well organized upper class was in power because they handled the importation of the materials and mastered the technology of the time, i.e. the casting of bronze. Members of this class were interred in oak coffins in large burial mounds. Their rich tombs also contain some of the oldest preserved everyday clothing in the world, woven from ox and sheep hair with ribbons of horse hair.

One of many indications of nature worship is the so-called "Sun Chariot", now in the National Museum, but as elsewhere in the Bronze Age a personification of the godly powers began to take place. Man created gods in his own image.

The climate of the Bronze Age was relatively dry and continental with warm summers. But towards the end of the period it changed to a more coastal, humid one with prevailing westerly winds from the Atlantic, rather like the climate of Denmark today. Together with this a new advance in technology, the coming of iron, once again revolutionized society.

The Iron Age (c. 500 B.C. – 750 A.D.)

Iron has a much higher melting point than bronze, but it is much more common in the ground, even in Danish bogs, so when the knowledge of concentrating fire to produce the temperature needed to melt iron reached Denmark at about 500 B.C., it replaced stone in everyday objects, such as knives. This metal was not a privilege for a limited class.

The new climatic conditions demanded more sophisticated ploughs and weeding tools as well as warmer clothes. After the first difficult adjustment, Iron Age people began to reap larger and better-quality crops of grain.

During the Iron Age large parts of the Danish landscape changed from forest to open farm land. In certain regions villages lay almost as close together as today, but cutting down the forests also meant that heaths began to spread over the poorer soils of western and central Jutland, whereas forests still covered large areas with more clayey soil as in the islands, and everywhere were swamps with brushwood. Excavations of villages seem to show that they were fenced in, perhaps against wolves for one reason.

9

The average village might contain a large farm with room for about 25 head of cattle, a dozen or more farms with room for about half the number of cattle as well as a number of small houses for artisans and workers without room for big animals. Houses were built of wood and clay with thatched roofs and a smoke-hole for the fireplace in the centre. In the farmbuildings people lived in one end and the animals in the other, and all buildings were oriented east-west as is the case of Danish farms even today.

The period from c. 500 B.C – 0 is often referred to as the "Celtic or pre-Roman Iron Age" which may be misleading, as neither the Celts nor the Romans ever dominated this region. The Celts included the Britons and the Gauls as well as peoples living near the Danube. They were all subdued by the Romans, while most of the Germanic tribes remained "barbarians" outside the Roman Empire.

The most striking find from this period in Denmark is the "Gundestrup Cauldron", a silver vessel of considerable size, 16 inches high and 28 inches in diameter with embossed decorations of religious processions, imaginary animals and a number of Celtic gods.

The time from c. 0 – 400 A.D. is known as the "Roman" part of the Iron Age, because the finds reflect the proximity of the Roman Empire, mainly luxury items as silver and bronze vessels and decorated glasses. Of a quite different kind are the famous "bog people", i.e. executed persons deposited in bogs in Jutland, for which reason some of these bodies were so well preserved that it was possible to take their fingerprints and analyze the contents of their stomachs. They were possibly outlaws, but the location might indicate religious sacrifices. Similar finds have been done in Holland and NW-Germany, but the two bodies, now in the museums of Silkeborg and Aarhus respectively, are among the best preserved.

Sacrifices to the gods in swampy areas took place from the Late Stone Age to the dawn of Christianity. Caesar and other Latin authors testify to this in their decriptions of the Germanic peoples. The most impressive of the bog finds are enormous heaps of weapons and war booty in Funen and Eastern Jutland dating from the time of the great migrations in Europe c. 200 – 500 A.D. It is doubtful how much the population of Denmark was affected by the migrations, but the finds may indicate battles between local inhabitants and invaders. The latter might have been the Danes pouring out of Zealand and the rest of Scandinavia, and the defeated the Angles and the Jutes who gradually settled in England together with the Saxons from Germany after the collapse of the Roman rule in England.

The last part of the Iron Age c. 400-750 A.D. is called "Germanic". After the fall of the Roman Empire and the migrations the Germanic peoples began to thrive, in Denmark reflected in the abundance of treasures of gold. A special Germanic style of art arose, and the alphabet, called the "Runic", began to spread. The majority of the oldest inscriptions in this alphabet have been found in and around Denmark, dating from c. 200 A.D. and onwards.

The climate became somewhat warmer than it is today, more land was farmed, and the population grew. The oldest one third of the present village names in Denmark date from this period, and these villages are still among the largest in size. A common prefix of their names is Thor-.

It is very fragmentary what we know of the old Nordic mythology. The ancestral god was Tyr, or Tio, etymologically the same word as Greek Zeus and Latin Deus (hence French Dieu), in English handed down in "Tuesday". By this time however Woden (cf. Wednesday) seems to have been the chief god, in the Viking Period even to be overshadowed by Thor (cf. Thursday), the god of thunder and fertility, whereas Freya (cf. Friday) was the goddess of fertility.

It is also uncertain when Denmark was organized as a nation. The first known name of a Danish king is that of *Hugleik*, who, according to a Frankish chronicle, fell in a naval attack on the Frankish north coast in 515 A.D. It is generally believed that the Old English epic Beowulf relates about Danish kings such as *Halvdan, Roar, Helge and Rolf*. As their names have also been preserved independently in Nordic legends and sagas, it is almost certain that they were real figures, probably kings in the 7th and 8th centuries, but whether they were national or only local kings is obscure.

The Viking Period

c. 750 – 1035 A.D.

The eighth century marks a turning point in European history. Christianity was consolidated and spreading. In 732 the Frankish leader, Charles Martel, thrust the Islamic invaders back across the Pyrenees. In the Rhine area trading and manufacturing centres grew up, and the Frisians settled and traded along the coast of the North Sea from Holland to Denmark. Now the two oldest towns of Denmark, Ribe and Hedeby, placed to the west and the east respectively of the narrow neck of South Jutland, began to grow up. Here goods were transported between the North Sea and the Baltic. From Hedeby, the forerunner of Slesvig (in German "Schleswig"), an important trade route developed to the Swedish trading centre of Birka, near present-day Stockholm, and further to the east.

To defend the vital link between the two seas a wall of earth and wood was erected near Hedeby, called "Danevirke" (i.e. "the Danes' work") at about 750. Its dimensions indicate that at this time Denmark, or at least most of it, was an organized state. This frontier-wall was soon to be threatened. Charlemagne (768-814) not only created the Frankish Empire, but also conquered and christianized the western part of present Germany in a series of bloody campaigns. In this long war Denmark was constantly a place of refuge for many German leaders and their men whom Denmark refused to deliver over to Charlemagne.

At the same time the first reports of Viking raids along the coasts of the North Sea appeared, thus the monastery on the island of Lindisfarne off the coast of Northumberland was plundered and set to fire in 793. The background to these raids may have been a combination of overpopulation, a lust for adventure and expansion as well as a reaction to the confrontation with a hostile and advancing Christian civilization. What made them possible was the construction of swift, flexible sailing ships, and a growing experience of day and night navigation.

There is no recognized explanation for the word "Viking". A Vik (or

Vig) is a creek, so perhaps the Vikings means simply the people who gathered their ships in creeks. In France they were known as Northmen or Normans, not Vikings.

In 810 Charlemagne planned an attack on Denmark, but refrained, because the Danevirke had been reinforced, and a Danish fleet attacked his Frisian provinces. In that year the Danish king *Godfred* was killed, but in the following year Charlemagne acknowledged the Eider River just to the south of the Danevirke as the frontier between Germany and Denmark, and so it stayed until 1864.

In 826 Christianity was preached on Danish soil for the first time, by a Frankish monk, Ansgar.

While the first Viking raids were sporadic, from 830 they took the form of well organized invasions, and reached more distant destinations. From Sweden Vikings crossed the Baltic, penetrated Russia and created the first towns and states on Russian soil (i.e. not counting the Ukraine). They established the 2000 mile long trade routes along the Dnieper and the Volga to the Arab world, from where they brought back such coveted items as swords and silk from Damascus.

The Norwegian Vikings settled the islands of the North Atlantic, the Shetlands, the Faroes and Iceland, and a hundred years later Greenland. They established a base on the Isle of Man and founded the first towns in Ireland, such as Dublin and Cork.

The most populous of all the settlements, however, were the Danish ones in Northern and Eastern England, finally established at about 870, while King Alfred the Great of Wessex gathered the southwestern half of England under his rule. The Danes organized their rule from fortified boroughs, and settled and farmed so much land that in large regions up to 50% of the place names are of Danish origin (such as names ending in -by (town), -toft (village), and -dale (valley). These regions were not ruled from Denmark, but administered according to traditional Danish law, for which reason the area was known as the Danelaw. The word "law" is of Scandinavian origin, and the roots of the jury system may be found in the Danelaw. As for language and religion the Danes gradually assimilated into their English surroundings and became Christians. The Scandinavians were never exclusive, and in Ireland as well as in Russia they married into local chieftains' families. First and foremost they were indefatigable traders, but handicrafts also flourished, as can be seen from recent excavations in York and Dublin.

In the middle of the ninth century Viking fleets twice ravaged faraway

13

Islamic cities as Lisbon and Seville. In Sicily they met compatriots who had arrived from the East via Constantinople. When the Frankish Empire was weakened and split up into France, Germany and Lorraine-Italy, France was destined to be the next target of the Scandinavian expansion. In 885 a siege of Paris was given up against ransom, but in the following decades more and more Northmen poured into Northern France in the "Grand Army", which is said to have numbered 40,000 people, no doubt including women and children.

In 911 an agreement was made between Charles the Simple of France and the Norman leader Rollo (who was undoubtedly Danish according to recent studies of primary sources) to settle the Grand Army in the area known as Normandy from that time. Here the Normans within a few generations adopted a form of French and became Christians. But they retained their own administration, and the dukes of Normandy were only nominally under the authority of the king of France, as was clearly seen in the events of 1066.

In the 10th century the Viking raids to the west died down due to a renewed German pressure on Denmark. In 934 Hedeby, the commercial nucleus and the main seat of the Danish kings, was conquered by the Germans, and in 948 missionary bishops were appointed to Hedeby and Ribe as well as to Aarhus, a town that had grown up since 900 on the east coast of Jutland behind a semi-circular rampart. However, the two latter probably never reached their destinations, because out of the blow to the former dynasty and the consequent internal strife, a new and very powerful dynasty emerged. It was founded by *Gorm "the Old"*, who might formerly have been one of the lords of the Danelaw in England.

The main road up through Jutland, called the Army Road, led from Hedeby to Viborg, Jutland's old meeting place and religious centre. It followed roughly the watershed, but midway it was only approx. 5 miles from the fjord of Vejle, part of the sea. Here at a place called Jelling (pronounced Yelling) King Gorm made his main seat, witnessed to this day by the two biggest burial mounds in Denmark and by two runic stones, one erected by Gorm and the other by his son *Harald "the Bluetooth"*. The later stone dating from the 960s, beautifully carved, reads: "Harald, the king, ordered this memorial made for his father Gorm and his mother Thyra, the Harald who won all of Denmark, and also Norway, and (made) the Danes Christians." It is called the certificate of baptism of the Danes, and the two stones may be considered the oldest historical documents in Denmark. Whereas the words "and also Norway" seem to have

14

been added after the decoration had been finished, by the words "all of Denmark" Harald wanted to stress the fact that he had regained control of the important Hedeby area. But the danger was far from over. In 962 the German king Otto was appointed "German-Roman Emperor" by the pope, which implied the Church's blessing on warfare against non-Christian countries. As a political realist Harald converted to Christianity, and commenced a complete reconstruction of the Danevirke in about 968. This was a tremendous engineering achievement for which tens of thousands of oak trees were felled. Nevertheless in 974 the Germans once more conquered Hedeby, so it may have been for reasons of security that Harald now exchanged his main seat of Jelling in Jutland for that of Roskilde in Zealand, which of course was also more centrally located for the entire kingdom, which included Scania (now part of Sweden).

In 981 Harald's son Svend or *Sweyn "the Forkbeard"* reconquered Hedeby, and firmly established his rule throughout Denmark. The three excavated viking camps and military strongholds of Trelleborg, Fyrkat and Aggersborg also date from just around 980. Sweyn was a representative of a new vigorous Viking generation trained in the battles with the Germans. As soon as the southern frontier was made secure, and the Germans diverted their desire for expansion to the Slav (or Slavic) peoples living in present East Germany, Sweyn directed his to England, which resulted in a second wave of viking raids on England, now organized as regular military expeditions.

In the 990s they were bought off against the Danegeld tax, but after 1000 a regular Danish army built up in England, and for a short time in 1013 it was in control of London, the key to the power of England. But shortly afterwards Sweyn died, and fights were resumed until in 1017 Sweyn's son Knud or *Canute "the Great"* was elected King of England by both Anglo-Saxons and Danes. Contrary to his father he was a convinced Christian, and rightly deserves the epithet "the Great". He reconciled the Anglo-Saxons and the Danes, pacified the Vikings, encouraged trade, religion and law, and became the real "christianizer" of Denmark. His reign extended to the Atlantic islands and Norway, but fell apart after his death in 1035, when he was only 40.

The Middle Ages

1035 – 1536

Early Christianity (c. 1035 – 1150)

Canute's reign concluded not only the Viking era, but also prehistory. With the coming of Christianity the growing number of literary sources written in Latin established history. The native runic alphabet, however, lingered on for centuries especially among artisans.

In Denmark Canute was succeeded by his son *Hardeknud*, but when he died in 1042, the Norwegian king *Magnus the Good*, son of "Saint" Olaf, was elected king of Denmark as well. In his time a new menace appeared: the heathen Wends, a Slav people living along the coast of the Baltic Sea south of Denmark. Strongly pressed by the Germans, they took up the Viking tradition of making raids – on Denmark. But in a great battle in 1043 on the heath north of Hedeby Magnus crushed a large Wendish invasion army.

After Magnus' death in 1047 the Danes chose *Svend Estridsen,* a son of Canute's sister Estrid as king. His reign 1047-74 became a period of prosperity and stability.

In spite of the emigrations from Denmark in the Viking Time, the home population had greatly increased, and the clearing of land was extensive though there was still no lack of wood for houses and ships. Judged from the village names another third of the Danish villages date from this time, and they are also considerable in size, whereas the latter third, founded c. 1050 – 1300, were mainly "thorps", i.e. satellites to the older villages. The ending -torp was in time corrupted into -rup, and the first part of these late village names are frequently of Christian origin, such as in common names as Pederstrup and Poulstrup.

With the spread of Christianity wooden churches were erected throughout the country in the 11th century. Unfortunately none of these have survived to our days. They were obviously placed centrally in the

The "Sun Chariot" from c. 1400 B.C., bronze, two feet long. The National Museum (p. 9).

Megalithic tomb called a cromlech or dolmen from approx. 3,500 B.C. At Stenvad, Djursland, E. Jutland (p. 8).

Burial ground of Lindholm Høje, N. Jutland. Ship-formed burials from the 9th century.
In the background the Limfjord and the city of Aalborg.

In the Viking Ship Museum at Roskilde, (Zealand), five ships of different types are being
reassembled out of 60,000 fragments.

villages on former cult or meeting places, sometimes built near or even on the top of ancient burial mounds. Altogether the conversion seems to have been peaceful. English monks founded the first monasteries such as St. Ben's at Ringsted in Zealand and St. Alban's at Odense in Funen ("Odense" means Wodin's High Place), and English mint-masters made the first Danish coins. The art of building in stone with mortar also reached Denmark by that route. Around 1030 Canute's sister, Estrid, had a stone church erected at Roskilde (predecessor of the present cathedral).

The English influence declined after the splitting up of Canute's empire and more so after 1066, as William the Conqueror looked upon Danes in and outside of England as the greatest danger to his power. Another reason was that the Danish gate to the west, the Limfjord, gradually sanded up at its North Sea end, and sailing north of the tip of Jutland was risky. So when in about 1060 the Church was organized in eight dioceses, they were officially placed under the archbishop of Hamburg. The crypt under Our Lady's Church at Aarhus must have been built as cathedral at this time, and is thus both the oldest preserved stone building and church in Denmark.

In the 11th century the Church was still in its beginning as an institution. People considered their local church as their own property, they paid for individual services, but refused to pay tithes. Nor was clerical jurisdiction and celibacy of priests accepted. However the pope forced King Svend to give up his marriage to a second cousin with the result that after that he had ever-changing concubines. The five of his many sons who succeeded him as kings, all had different mothers.

When Svend died in 1074 he was a popular and respected king although he had not reached his highest aim of creating a national church free from foreign sovereignty.

After his death we can distinguish for the first time the contours of political groupings, which we might call traditionalists and centralists. The latter were made up by a warrior caste, the embryo of the aristocracy, trained in Viking raids across the Baltic on the Wends, and who wanted a stronger, centralized rule working hand in hand with the Church. But the bulk of the population, the traditionalists, only wanted to live and farm peacefully, clinging to the old laws, so at a meeting of all the boatsmen of Denmark they elected Svend's oldest son *Harald*, whom our oldest history writers, because they were ecclesiastics, gave the epithet *"the Soft"*. He clarified the laws and issued good coins contrary to his centralist brother *"Saint" Knud*, who seized the power without election

17

on the death of Harald in 1080. Knud raised the taxes, confiscated much land and gave a good share of it to the Church. Thus the oldest Danish document known *in extenso* is that of a donation from him to the bishop of Lund in Scania, dated 1085. Twice he planned to reconquer England, but he never carried out his plan. The second time the people rioted and killed him at Odense in 1086. According to the chroniclers he was slain right in front of the altar of St. Alban's, which helped to get him sanctified (see below). His successor, the traditionalist *Olaf "Hunger"* had the misfortune to reign when much of Northern Europe was stricken by famine. At his death in 1095 the centralists managed to get their candidate, the fourth brother, *Erik "the Ever Good"* elected because of their convincing arguments that the famine was God's punishment, and that miracles had taken place at Knud's grave. However, he first had to swear that he would keep the old law, meaning no doubt that he would refrain from new taxes. Nevertheless he found means for an attack on the Wendish island of Rügen which he laid under tribute. After that he went to Rome, where he had his brother Knud sanctified, and obtained the pope's appointment of a Scandinavian archbishop at Lund, effected shortly after 1100. Later when Norway and Sweden had their own archbishops, the Danish one remained at Lund although the natural place would have been Roskilde. This was a factor that helped to segregate Scania (which was finally lost to Sweden in 1658) from the rest of the country. As a national state Denmark's greatest problem was always that it consisted of separated regions: Jutland, the islands and Scania.

In 1099 Jerusalem had been conquered in the first crusade, and a few years later Erik set out on a pilgrimage, leaving the petty local problems in the hands of his earls. He chose the usual Scandinavian route, which was to sail up the Dvina and down the Dnieper. He visited the emperor of Byzantium, but died in the island of Cyprus before reaching the Holy Land in 1103.

Under the peaceful traditionalist *King Niels (1104-34),* the last of the five brothers to become king, Denmark experienced 25 years of great progress, in which time the erection of stone churches began to spread all over the country. Quite a few had been built even before the turn of the century, but they were built of relatively soft kinds of stone such as limestone, which was only available to a very limited degree. Now the builders turned to the hard and coarse granite of glacial boulders, plentiful in most parts of the country. This was unique in Europe. Within approximately 100 years some 1200 granite churches were erected together with about 300 of other stones in present-day Denmark. This is one of the greatest achievements the Danes ever performed, and the old stone churches may be our greatest cultural treasure.

Only along the coasts of the Baltic Sea there is an absence of stone churches because Wendish raids made life insecure here. The centralists accused Niels of neglecting defence, mocking him because he travelled with only seven men, called "housecarls", one being his chancellor (secretary), one his marshall (horseman and military leader) and one his treasurer – in reality the beginning of royal administration.

The most complex question in the history of Denmark is that of the Danish-German border (the Slesvig issue). The reason why it became so intricate can only be understood if we look at what happened in this region in the days of King Niels.

At about 1000 Hedeby was burnt down, possibly by the Wends, and was moved to a more secure place on the north side of the fjord and named Slesvig.

Like Hedeby, Slesvig became the biggest town in Denmark, so important that its name began to be used as a term for the whole region of South Jutland.

At about 1115 Niels appointed his nephew, Knud Lavard (Lord), son of Niels' predecessor, King Erik, as earl of South Jutland, where this brilliant young man carried out his own policy. To combat the Wends he entered into an alliance with Germany, acknowledging the German emperor as his feudal lord, thus being at the same time a Danish earl and a German duke. With this he introduced feudalism into Denmark. He invited a great number of Germans into his province, not only clerks, tradesmen and artisans, but also peasants to clear the forests and settle in the southeastern corner as a buffer to the Wends.

At Christmas 1130 the old King Niels gathered all the leading Danes at Roskilde. According to German sources all of them, including the king and the archbishop, looked like Nordic peasants, dressed as they were in homespun wool, whereas Knud glittered in silk and purple. A fortnight later Niels' son Magnus killed Knud, his cousin and rival to the throne, as Niels was about 70 years old. The people clearly sided with the king, but the centralists obtained reinforcements in the form of German cavalry that crushed the Danish army. Magnus and five of the eight bishops fell. This was probably the first time that professional, mounted horsemen went to battle in Denmark. Shortly afterwards King Niels was killed by Knud's followers in the town of Slesvig.

The period from 1131 to 1157 was politically unstable due to the many pretenders to the throne, all descendants of Svend Estridsen and his five royal sons. This political vacuum gave Eskil, archbishop of Lund 1138-77, a welcome chance to bring his Church up to European standards in power and influence. Eskil worked in close contact with his teacher and friend, Bernhard of Clairvaux, who wanted to make the Church independent of any temporal power ("Gregorianism"). Eskil introduced canonical law and founded a number of monasteries of Bernhard's new reform-order, the Cistercians. In Lund he had his own large stone cathedral inaugurated in 1145. The similar Romanesque stone cathedrals of Ribe and Viborg were also built in the 12th century, the latter being totally renewed in the 19th century.

As the German colonization of the Slav areas to the east continued, the Wends took advantage of the fact that Denmark was torn by internal strife. They made raids and even established settlements especially in the islands of Lolland and Falster, south of Zealand. In 1143 the Germans reached the Baltic Sea and founded Lübeck, which was to become the commercial centre of the Baltic with the consequence that Slesvig began to decline.

The Glorious Period of The Valdemars (1157 – 1241)

A renewed civil war among throne pretenders came to an end in 1157, when *Valdemar I "the Great"* assumed sole power at the age of 26. As son of Knud Lavard and Ingeborg of Novgorod in Russia he was given a Danish version of the Russian Vladimir as name. Born one week after his father was killed in 1131, he was protected and raised in the home of Asser Rig, head of the richest and most influential family in Zealand, the Hvide family, together with Asser's two own sons, Esbern and Absalon.

To conciliate the traditionalists Valdemar married a daughter of Magnus, his father's murderer, and to further consolidate his rule he placed his adherents in key positions, first of all, Absalon, 29, who had studied theology in Paris, in the bishop's seat at Roskilde in 1158. This infringement on eccleciastical investiture was possible because just at this time the German emperor Frederick Barbarossa was holding archbishop Eskil in custody. He had been seized on his way back from Rome. This brought about the century-long European strife between Church and State, but Eskil himself was soon after released.

Having become firmly established at about 1160 Valdemar turned his interest to the long neglected defence of the country. Once more the Danevirke was renewed, this time in brick, which was an innovation here, and a network of stone fortresses were laid across the country. All of these were strategically well placed: Sønderborg (borg = castle) to guard the Baltic coast of South Jutland as well as the southern entrance of the Little Belt; Nyborg, Sprogø and Korsør to make a defence line across the Great Belt; Vordingborg in southern Zealand, from where ships could operate in the narrow waters around the very exposed islands south of Zealand. In 1167 Absalon was commissioned to build the first castle at Copenhagen on the east coast of Zealand to guard the Sound while his brother Esbern founded Kalundborg on the west coast of the same island.

At Ringsted, the old meeting place of Zealand, Valdemar erected a burial church for his dynasty in connection with the old monastery of St. Ben (see page 17). This is the oldest preserved brick building in Denmark. It was consecrated at a great ceremony in 1170 on which occasion a treaty was made between the King and the Church. Valdemar's father, Knud Lavard, was sanctified, and Valdemar's son, also named Knud, was crowned as (future) king. With the coronation by the archbishop the Church obtained veto power in this matter, and thus Valdemar put an end to the popular elections of kings. In future the people only had to give homage to the new king. From then Valdemar used the term "by grace of God king of Denmark", and adopted as the coat of arms three blue lions in a yellow field with little red hearts, which is still the emblem of Denmark.

Certain architectural details in the apse of the church of Ringsted suggest that it was Italians who first taught the Danes to make tiles and build in this artificial "stone", which in time was to become one of the most characteristic features of Denmark.

Absalon soon followed in the steps of his master, King Valdemar, and founded a Cistercian monastery at Sorø, 10 miles west of Ringsted, and commenced its brick abbey which similarly was to be the burial place of *his* family, while his brother Esbern was responsible for the erection of the unique church of Kalundborg in the shape of a Greek cross with five towers. In 1177 Absalon succeeded Eskil as archbishop. About this time his clerk, Saxo "Grammaticus" completed his voluminous "Gesta Danorum" ("The Deeds of the Danes"), the first history of Denmark, written in learned and flowery Latin, full of legends and sagas with vivid descriptions of spectacular battles, etc., but highly biased, seen as it is from a centralist point of view. Shakespeare's Hamlet is based on a story from this.

As an ever growing number of local stone churches were completed, a good deal of them were decorated with costly wall paintings, possibly executed by French artists. The high standard of Danish handicraft at the time is seen not only from stone sculptures of the churches and their baptismal fonts, but also from the "golden altars", made of embossed and gilt copperplates.

Towards the end of the century the present brick cathedral of Roskilde began to take the place of its stone predecessor. It represents a transitional style from the Romanesque to the Gothic.

It was not until the turn of the twelfth century that a brick building was commenced in Jutland with the cathedral of Aarhus. This reflects the fact that Zealand had now taken over from Jutland the role of the leading province, politically, economically and culturally. Zealand was not only the geographical centre of the country, but also Valdemar's political base. Here large forests, especially in North Zealand, now provided room for new settlers. But the eastward move of the country's centre of gravity had also important external reasons. As we have seen sea trade to the west, especially to England declined, while Christianity and trade expanded eastward in Europe. As Lübeck assumed the former role of Slesvig, ships began to prefer the Sound to the Great Belt, which also explains why Copenhagen began to grow faster than the other towns.

Copenhagen's main industry was fishing and the export of salted herring. From the rest of the country grain was the main export, while salt, iron and wine were imported. Towns grew up at the end of every fjord, where land and sea transport naturally meet. In the 13th century these towns were provided with brick churches, and so were the rural districts where Slav penetration had formerly prevented the erection of stone churches, e.g. the islands of Lolland and Falster. An important new phenomenon in the towns were the black and grey friars. Considering that the founders of these "mendicant orders", St. Dominicus and St. Francis of Assisi died in 1221 and in 1226 respectively it is remarkable that the first monasteries of their orders were founded as early as in 1223 and 1232 respectively in Danish towns, where they began social and educational work.

The biggest town was Ribe, Denmark's port to the southwest with perhaps 4000 inhabitants, where great works were undertaken in the 13th century. A dam, which is now the main street of the town, was constructed across the river with water mills, and ramparts and moats were established around the town. Most of its houses were of wood.

The oldest preserved *secular* brick building in Denmark is the lower part of the castle of Nyborg in Funen, built at the beginning of the 13th century as a royal castle for the king's meetings with the lords. Most of these still lived in wooden houses, whereas the peasants' farms were increasingly constructed in half-timbering, i.e. a framework of wood filled in with wattle and daub to save wood which was now less plentiful because of the growing population and the demand for fuel, especially for the baking of bricks. Roofs were of thatch with holes for the smoke from the fireplace on the ground.

King Valdemar the Great was succeeded by his two sons, *Knud VI* 1182-1202 and *Valdemar II "the Victorious"* 1202-1241. All three kings turned the Slav raids on Denmark into Danish "crusades" across the Baltic. During the conquest of Estonia in 1219 the Danish flag with the white cross on a red bunting is said to have dropped from heaven. In reality the use of it can only be testified from about 150 years later, but even so it is considered the oldest of present-day European flags.

For a time Valdemar II even became overlord of the provinces along the south coast of the Baltic, the former Slav areas now colonized by the Germans, but in 1223 one of the king's German vassals kidnapped him and kept him in prison for three years until he was finally ransomed. In 1227 the Danish army was crushed by the Germans who clearly showed whose sphere of interest the Baltic coast was. Denmark had neither the resources of people or money for a grand scale colonization to match the Germans. What was left of this short-lived Danish empire was a certain dominance of the island of Rügen and the country of Estonia, whose capital has two names – Reval and Talinn, the latter meaning the Danish city.

In the long absence of the king no riots broke out, no pretenders to the throne appeared, and no strife arose among bishops and lords. All this shows how strong the royal authority had become. As a wounded and now one-eyed king, having also lost his beloved Queen Dagmar (originally a Czech princess, Dragomir) as well as their only son, Valdemar II proved to be a truly great king, now concentrating on internal affairs. In 1231 a cadaster of land was made out (a parallel to William the Conqueror's Domesday Book), which proves the high level of administration. Many of the former duties to the king had been replaced by land taxation.

Under Knud VI the regional laws of Zealand and Scania had been written down in the runic letters, and in 1241, shortly before his death, Valdemar II signed the Lawbook of Jutland, also written in Danish, but in Latin letters. As such it is the most extensive text in Danish from the Middle Ages. In the preamble it says that the base of society is law, and that the law is to protect the weak and the peaceful, and must be so clear that everybody can understand it. "The law is given by the king and consented to by the people. The king executes the law. He is only responsible to God ..." (i.e. not to the Church). The law affirms that the land is the king's, whereas hitherto the traditionalists had maintained that the land belonged to those who settled it.

As a matter of interest it may be mentioned that the law contains the first treasure trove provision in any European code, stating simply that gold and silver found in the ground and claimed by nobody belonged to the king.

The bulk of the law concerns itself with the individual and his rights, contrary to other continental laws of the time, which were state-centred. There is a complete absence of the otherwise obligatory harsh punishments meted out to people who committed lese-majesty ("crimen majestatis"). On the whole it is very humane for its time, which may explain its long life. In the 16th century it was printed and its validity extended to all of Denmark. Large parts of it were transferred to the second great code of 1683. In the province of Slesvig it was the basic law until 1900 when it was replaced by Prussian law.

The Jutland Law was the finest flower of the Valdemarian Period, but seen with hindsight it is clear that only Valdemar II's firm rule had kept problems at bay. His Baltic warfare had cost a lot of money, and in the last years of his reign inflation was growing. Everywhere in Europe countries were shaken and torn apart in the strife between Church and State and between the kings and the vassals. The fundamental causes may have been a slightly colder climate and a general demoralization in Europe as the political manipulation of the crusades became evident.

The bishops had loyally cooperated with Valdemar, but when would new church leaders demand supremacy over the state and claim complete exemption from taxes to the state? (Land acquired by the churches and the monasteries prior to 1215 was taxfree, which of course only an efficient royal administration could control.)

But it was cavalry, the new mode of warfare, which really changed society. Because of the enormous expense of equipping armoured horsemen, warfare became a matter for specialists, and a warrior class among the big land owners arose, the beginning of an aristocratic class. In return for their military services they (i.e. their land) were tax-free, whereas all others paid heavy defence-taxes instead of doing military service. This meant for one thing that the defence line of Danevirke became worthless as it needed to be manned in its full extent. More serious was the fact that peasants began to see an advantage in selling their land to the local warlord and become leaseholders, which meant that the revenue of the state dwindled.

Cavalry also favoured feudalism, which again endangered the unity of a country. A vassal's fief was originally strictly personal between him and the king, but soon vassals built up their own power and tried to make the fiefs hereditary. Valdemar II had three sons from his second marriage, and he made them dukes of various parts of Denmark which resulted in internal strife.

Decline and Fall of Denmark (1241 - 1340)

This period is the most sinister chapter of Danish history. After the death of Valdemar II in 1241 a monk noted: "With his death the crown truly dropped from the head of the Danes; now they began fighting among themselves and destroying one another."

Soon after Valdemar's oldest son *Erik*, 25, had become king, it was evident that he lacked his father's authority. In his short reign 1241-50 he managed to clash with his brothers, the bishops and the people. Immediately a war broke out with his brother Abel, duke of Slesvig, who married a daughter of the neighbouring German count of Holstein and invited German lords to be sub-vassals in his dukedom.

The increased war-taxes made the bishops complain to the pope after which the bishop of Roskilde was accused of plotting against the state. He saved his own life by fleeing to Clairvaux in France.

In 1249 when Erik presented a new tax, a penny on each plough, at Lund, the Scanians revolted, but were suppressed, but to posterity the king was known as "Erik the Plough-Penny".

In 1250 under a visit to Abel's town of Slesvig Erik was seized and killed. The next day fishermen found his body in the fjord. (It was in the same town that King Niels had been murdered in 1134).

Now the unbelievable happened. *Abel* rushed to Viborg and swore that he had had no hand in the murder – and was elected king. Perhaps this was seen as the only chance to reunite Denmark and Slesvig and to re-establish peace, which Abel also did for a while. But his problem was the same as that of his brother, lack of means, so in 1252 he made a tax raid on the Frisians along the west coast of South Jutland. They acknowledged the Danish king as their overlord, but paid practically no tributes. But Abel's army was defeated, and he fell in a battle near Husum in 1252.

Very conveniently for the third brother *Christoffer,* Abel's son was held for ransom by the archbishop of Cologne, which was not an unusual thing in this time of greed and disorder when many bishops operated like other lords with their own armies. Christoffer now became king, but Abel's son was ransomed by his uncles, the counts of Holstein, who forced Christoffer to give him his father's dukedom of Slesvig, which in reality became a heriditary fief with the dukes as puppets of the counts of the much bigger and richer German Holstein. A customs frontier grew up between North and South Jutland (the latter equal to the province of Slesvig). The segregation of this old Danish province hereby took an important step.

The same may be said about the eastern province of Scania. Here Christoffer's personal enemy, the archbishop of Lund, Jacob Erlandsen, vehemently claimed clerical jurisdiction, and began to build strongholds, the most important of which was the Hammershus Castle in the island of Bornholm (today Denmark's biggest ruin).

In various parts of the country peasant riots broke out, but they were brutally suppressed. In this matter all the lords could agree, but to secure the lords' support the king yielded them a greater control of the royal power and revenue. Christoffer was no doubt a talented politician, but all odds were against him, and his reign so short that he never got a chance. In 1259 he died so suddenly that rumours arose to the effect that he had been poisoned while receiving communion in the cathedral of Ribe, a rumour which is nonetheless highly doubtful.

His widow queen Margrethe pressed the bishop of Viborg to crown their minor son *Erik V.* In renewed battles with Holstein both Margrethe and Erik were captured, and the country dissolved into a state of anarchy. Towns, monasteries and farms were plundered by royal, ducal and episcopal gangs, and the country was placed under a papal interdict.

After his release Erik, who came of age at about 1267, gradually resumed royal power, and the interdict was raised in 1275. But because of the military expenses the aristocrats made him transfer all the remaining royal dues on their leaseholders to them with a catastrophic result for the revenue. Now his coin-masters began to "clip" metal from the coins, hence Erik's nickname, "Klipping".

In 1282 at a state meeting at the castle of Nyborg the lords forced Erik to sign the first Charter of Denmark. It institutionalized an annual "parlamentum", introduced a habeas corpus act, and transferred much of the royal jurisdiction to the regional courts which the local lords controlled. This has been called the first constitution of Denmark, but it had little to do with what we understand by democracy. Its aim was only to improve the power of the new aristocratic class at the expense of that of the king. In 1284 the aristocratic opposition was so strong that it could install its leaders in the government, placing the king under direct control.

In 1285 the duke of Slesvig made an open revolt, but was captured, and only got his dukedom back on humiliating conditions.

In 1286 King Erik was murdered near Viborg under mysterious circumstances (the last regicide in Denmark). His widow immediately made an alliance with the duke of Slesvig and had the aristocratic leaders sentenced for the murder. Most of them fled to Norway from where they made pirate attacks on Danish towns for many years to come. Common sense tells us that they had nothing to gain from a murder of the king whom they had just subjected to complete political control. All indications point to the duke of Slesvig as the man behind the murder.

Such dramatic and mysterious acts inspired writers of ballads, of which Denmark has a great treasure. They might even have been used as means of propaganda, but most of them were probably written at later times, when minstrels sang them while people danced chain dances and repeated the refrains.

After the murder of Erik Klipping his 12-year-old son, *Erik VI* with the inexplicable epithet of "Menved", became king. His early years became a repetition of his father's, only the archbishop now, Jens Grand, was an even more fanatic advocate of the Church's independence. Having come of age Erik imprisoned him, and once more Denmark was under a papal ban.

This was a period of complete disorder in Europe. The Hundred Years' War destroyed France, while Italy was torn by the Guelfs and the Ghibellines. In 1309 the pope fled to Avignon, and Germany was also in a state of dissolution due to the vassals' growing independence. Erik took advantage of this and resumed Valdemar II's venture to expand Danish sovereignty of Baltic areas, but to pay for this he handed over to German vassals ever growing parts of Denmark.

After his death in 1319 this development accelerated under his brother, *Christoffer II,* who died a beggar and a complete "Lackland" (i.e without land) in 1332. At this time Danish coin-making had stopped, and from 1332 to 1340 there was no king of Denmark. However the Holstein counts had *their* vassals and sub-vassals, who behaved like local kings obeying nobody, with the result that Denmark was now in a state of complete lawlessness. Copenhagen was a nest of pirates, and riots of impoverished peasants took place every year.

In this period of decline, 1241-1340, the founding of new villages came to a standstill, which lasted until about 1860, when new railway junctions began to grow up. Few cultural monuments are preserved from the period. The cathedral of Roskilde was finished c. 1270, and the equally beautiful abbey of Løgumkloster in South Jutland in the same transitional style was concluded c. 1325, probably never reaching its intended length. The truly Gothic cathedral of Odense was commenced at the end of the 13th century, and finished a hundred years later after the country had been re-organized.

The almost complete absence of wall paintings, etc., from this period, also reflect the miserable state of the country. The new class of lords erected small strongholds of stone or brick, but none have survived to this day. After a suppressed riot the peasants were forced to build a royal castle at Kalø near Aarhus at 1314, but the impressive ruin is mainly remnants of later days.

Re-establishment of Denmark and Nordic Union
(1340 – 1448)

In the year of 1340 a war of liberation broke out. At this time the clever, but ruthless Holstein count Gerhard "the Bald" was the master of Jutland, and his cousin Johan "the Mild" was overlord of the islands, whereas the Scanians had rioted and asked for protection of Sweden.

In the winter of 1340 Gerhard was on a raid in Jutland to amass silver, but during his stay at the town of Randers on the night of April 1st a young Danish squire, Niels Ebbesen, in a very well planned assault managed to get into his headquarters, kill him and escape with his followers. This became the signal for riots all over Jutland. Soon Gerhard's army dissolved, and just at this moment king Christoffer II's youngest son *Valdemar* appeared from a stay at the court of the German emperor.

Now the Hanseatic League, which consisted of mainly German trade cities with Lübeck as its head put pressure on the Holstein counts to re-establish peace in the Danish waters with the consequence that Valdemar IV was acknowledged as king. He was a tall and strong person of extraordinary political talents, whose reign 1340-75 became one long struggle to re-establish Denmark. As a dowry of his marriage to a sister of the duke of Slesvig, a puppet of the Holstein counts, he received the northernmost part of Jutland, but his base became Zealand, which was less impoverished, and where the Church and the people made great sacrifices to pay for an army. Even after three years Valdemar had not conquered one castle from the vassal lords, but at popular meetings at Ringsted he appealed to the people, giving detailed accounts of what he had spent the money for. In the late 1340s his sieges of the castles in the islands were crowned with success until 1349-50 all activities were paralyzed as the Black Death reached Denmark. This bubonic plague originating in Asia killed off ¼ to ⅓ of all Europeans, also in Denmark.

By the 1350s Valdemar had resumed his Zealand policy in Jutland and gradually reinforced the old Danish laws. But now many local Jutland lords had also acquired a taste for independence from royal power so that they too had to be "pacified". In 1360 Valdemar took back Scania from Sweden, but this war went on, and in 1361 in a terrible massacre he conquered the Baltic island of Gotland whose main town of Visby was a member of the Hanseatic League. This led to a Hanseatic conquest of Copenhagen in 1368 where the old castle was demolished by stonemasons from Lübeck, while the Holstein counts reconquered Jutland. For a while everything that Valdemar had built up seemed lost, but a league of 37 otherwise peaceful trading cities stretching from Cologne in the west to Königsberg in the east was not made for a long war. Its main interest was to secure free passage through the Sound and gain economic control of the herring fishing there. In 1370 Valdemar handed over to the League the control of the castles on the Scanian side of the Sound together with a great share of the herring taxes there, both for a period of 15 years, to get peace in order to have a free hand in Jutland, which he once more cleared of Holstein domination.

Everything looked very bright for Valdemar in 1375 on this front because the last of the puppet dukes of Slesvig died without heirs so that South Jutland should rightly fall back to the king. But before this happened, Valdemar himself died at the age of 55.

The Holstein counts were in no way prepared to give up the province of Slesvig because their puppet duke had died. After 134 years of German penetration the German language had spread, especially in and around the town of Slesvig itself, and the Holstein counts were now proprietors of large parts of the land of the province.

King Valdemar IV came down in history as Valdemar "Atterday", meaning "New Day", and it is close to a miracle that he managed to re-create the Danish state. But the country was far from the prosperity of the time of the first Valdemars. Economically Denmark had become a satel-lite of the Hanseatic League which now controlled all the exports, es-pecially the fishing industry. The centre of this was at the southwestern corner of Scania where every autumn more than 20,000 people fished, cleaned, dried and salted herring to meet the demands of the growing European market due to the ever increasing fasting, imposed by the Church (in the 15th century four days of the week were meatless). Danish people did the manual work, but the Hanseatics furnished the barrels and the salt (from Lüneburg, south of Hamburg), handled the sale and pock-eted the profit.

The effect of the Black Death was that large parts of the sandy central and western parts of Jutland were more or less depopulated. Villages were deserted, churches fell into ruin, and the heather spread. People went to the more fertile eastern parts of the country, where the price of labour went up. Many of the survivors became richer by inheriting property, clothes and valuables. At this time Paris became the centre of fashion, which began to change increasingly. Few everyday clothes from Europe in the Middle Ages have survived. An exception is the specimens pre-served in the permafrost in Greenland (now in the National Museum of Copenhagen). They prove that the Scandinavians living there were in yearly contact with Europe as late as in the 14th and 15th centuries.

Even after his death the restless king Valdemar "New Day" was not allowed to rest in peace. He was first buried at Vordingborg in South Zea-land, his main military base, and where he had enlarged the castle im-mensely. His "Goose Tower" is still intact. But later his daughter Mar-grethe had his body transferred to the abbey of Sorø. In between these two places is Næstved, the trading centre of South Zealand, where the church of St. Peter has a wall painting representing the king, perhaps the first attempt of a portrait in Denmark.

When Valdemar died in 1375 without male heirs, he left the country in great confusion. In the following year, however, the state council elected his grandson, the 5-year-old Oluf, king. He was a son of Valdemar's youngest daughter Margrethe, married to King Haakon VI of Norway. In reality, *Margrethe* (born in 1353) became the ruling queen, while her husband remained in Norway.

To secure support from the Church she handed Copenhagen over to the bishop of Roskilde. All the other towns, including Roskilde, belonged to the king, and their citizens had always been the king's most loyal supporters. Ever since Copenhagen had been founded in 1167 by Bishop Absalon it had belonged to his episcopal successors, but Valdemar had reconquered it from the Germans in the 1340s, and had refused to hand it back to the bishop.

In 1380 Margrethe's husband died, leaving Oluf the crown of Norway. From then on a union between Denmark and Norway existed until 1814. With Norway came the Orkney, Shetland and Faroe Islands, Iceland and Greenland, but this "North Atlantic empire" was nothing like what it had been in the Viking era with its warmer climate. Since that time even Norway's population was probably halved. In the 15th century the Norse people in Greenland lost contact with Europe and died out. The annexation of Norway however, greatly improved Margrethe's prestige.

In contrast to her father Margrethe was a master of diplomacy and always eager to reach peaceful solutions, but in 1385 she showed that she mastered other means as well. As it became evident that the Hanseatic League was not prepared to hand back the Scanian castles as stipulated in 1370, piracy in the Sound suddenly increased. Because the League was not ready for a new war, it reluctantly ceded the castles, after which pirateering miraculously stopped again.

Immediately after her father's death the Holstein counts had taken military control of South Jutland (Slesvig). In 1386 she accepted this *fait accompli* as she had now her hands full of problems, this time in Sweden, which had undergone a parallel, though somewhat delayed, development to that of Denmark. In 1364 the great lords, tired of royal overlordship and taxation, had thrown out Haakon's father who had been king of both Sweden and Norway, and invited a German duke from Mecklenburg to take his place. Now almost a generation later they were equally tired of his abuses so that the Swedish state council secretly promised Margrethe that it would make her son Oluf king. But in 1387 Oluf died, after which there were no legal rights for Margrethe anywhere.

However, only a week after Oluf's death Margrethe was sworn in as "Denmark's proxy and guardian". Margrethe solved the problem of legality by adopting Erik, a 6-year-old grandson of her eldest sister, who was otherwise to inherit some small estates in Pomerania in NE-Germany. From now on he was brought up personally by Margrethe, and was soon acknowledged heir of Norway by the Norwegian council in Oslo, with his "mother" as regent. The following year the Swedish council followed suit. Its desire to get rid of the Mecklenburg duke must have been very intense, because it agreed to hand over to Margrethe all the main castles of Sweden, which she claimed necessary to re-establish law and order.

After some years of warfare practically all of Sweden was under Margrethe's rule, and in 1396 all three countries officially appointed Erik, now 14, king. In the following year at the castle of Kalmar in southern Sweden an inter-nordic meeting made out a draft for a Nordic union, but Margrethe kept it back, retaining power for herself as long as she lived.

Thanks to Margrethe the holy Birgitte (Bridget) of Vadstena, who had been related to the most influential Swedish families and had died at 1373, was sanctified. Her convent at Vadstena became a Nordic cultural centre. In Denmark Margrethe laid the economic basis for two nunneries of St. Bridget's order: Mariager in NE Jutland, whose church has been much reduced, and Maribo in Lolland, whose beautiful church was erected c. 1410-70, and which is now a cathedral. The names indicate the increased cult of the Virgin in the Late Middle Ages.

Step by step Margrethe carried through a great reduction of the power of the lords in Denmark. An efficient administration, led by her chancellor, Bishop Lodehat of Roskilde, dug out documents from old chests proving that much land in the years of disorder had been taken illegally from the crown. The transfer of many leaseholders back to royal taxation improved finances so much that it was possible to resume coin-making in 1396 after 60 years of suspension.

Many aristocratic strongholds were demolished, and in 1396 the erection of new ones was simply forbidden. This did not, however, prevent Bishop Lodehat from building the castle of Gjorslev in SE-Zealand, which still stands. Disputes with the lords were settled by royal courts whose power was unchallenged to such a degree that not a single lord rioted.

Now only one problem remained: Slesvig, Denmark's gate to the continent was said still to be out-of-joint, i.e. it was still under German rule. A chance of interfering in this region was cleverly intercepted by Margrethe when the count of Holstein died in 1404. Soon she was the master of the castles of the northern parts of the province, but in 1412 open fights

Apse of Staby Church in W. Jutland. Mainly in granite. 12th century.

Vejlby Curch, W. Funen, a typical Danish village church. Original parts in stone from the 12th cent. (p. 18-19). Additions in brick from 15th cent. (p. 18, 19, 35).

Baptismal font of granite, Vamdrup Church in S. Jutland. 12th cent.

Detail of granite portal, Vejlby Church, Allingaabro, E. Jutland. Late 12th cent.

Gothic wall painting from c. 1400. Tirsted Church, Island of Lolland.

broke out over the control of Flensborg, now the leading commercial centre of the area whereas the town of Slesvig was still the religious and administrative centre. The Danish army led by Erik was victorious, and in the autumn Margrethe made her entry into the battered town. An epidemic began to spread, and one of its victims was Margrethe herself, who died on a ship in the fjord at the age of 59. Once more a Danish sovereign had died just at the moment of regaining this old Danish province, and this was to be the final opportunity.

Margrethe's body was taken to Sorø, but soon afterwards Bishop Lodehat forcibly brought it to Roskilde, where the choir of the cathedral was made into a memorial to her.

If Valdemar "New Day" had given back to the Danish people the hope of peace and justice, his daughter had made it into reality. Whereas Valdemar was remembered in dramatic ballads as the wild hunter and passionate lover, the memory of Margrethe was passed down among people in more prosaic legends relating how she secured fields and meadows for the use of the citizens' cattle, by riding around the towns, marking out their limits, etc.

Margrethe never attained the official title of Queen of Denmark though nobody deserved it more. She was truly our greatest "statesman", and in our history she is always named "Queen Margrethe I" (1375-1412).

Danes have always liked pictures on their walls. From about 1360 the rich tradition of wall paintings in the churches was resumed. Fine examples of this "High Gothic" style are found in village churches such as Højby in NW-Zealand and Birkerød north of Copenhagen.

Erik VII "of Pomerania" was a man of great vision, but he lacked his great-aunt Margrethe's patience. As soon as he had taken over in 1412, he declared the fief of Slesvig forfeit, which led to an endless war with Holstein, and from now on the bishop's seat of Slesvig was consistently occupied by a German.

With this war still going on Erik ventured into the great project of concentrating his power around the Sound, the main entrance of the Baltic. First, after the death of Bishop Lodehat, he confiscated Copenhagen (see page 31), and installed himself in its castle, making this city the capital of Denmark from 1417. North of Copenhagen where the Sound is less than three miles wide he founded the castle of Elsinore (Helsingør), which was furnished with cannons, and the town was laid out according to a strict plan and supplied with two monasteries and a convent. On the opposite coast of the Sound he reinforced the castle of Helsingborg (where the old tower probably dates from his time), and erected castles at Landskrona and Malmø.

Everywhere Erik curbed the rights of the Hanseatics in order to transfer trade back into Danish hands, but what enraged the League and caused it to open a new war was his introduction of the Sound Toll in about 1425. This time, however, an attack on Copenhagen was beaten off by his queen Philippa, a daughter of Henry IV of England, so that from 1429 any ship passing into the Baltic had to pay a silver coin, officially to keep the waters free of piracy.

In Norway and Sweden there was no understanding of the need of increased war taxes. An uprising in Sweden led to Erik's defeat in the state councils. In 1438 he left Denmark forever, declaring that he did not want to be the "yes man" of the great lords.

His nephew, *Christoffer III "of Bavaria"*, 23, was offered the crowns in 1439. The Nordic union was re-established, but now with very limited royal power. The Hanseatics had their old privileges reconfirmed, and the duchy of Slesvig was handed over to the German count of Holstein, who from that time was also a Danish duke!

Now Denmark was back to aristocratic rule, and the peasants knew what that meant. Riots broke out both in Denmark and Sweden, the most serious one in North Jutland in 1441, but they were crushed by armed cavalry. After only nine years of rule Christoffer died in 1448, and with him the old royal line had died out.

Denmark in the Late Middle Ages (1448 – 1536)

The 15th century was a time of progress in Europe. After the decimation of the population in the 14th century it began to grow again. However, at about 1450 the total population of Denmark, including Scania and Slesvig, hardly reached one million, and that of Norway hardly ¼ mill. The area farmed in Denmark was smaller than that in the Valdemarian Period, but growing. Each planted seed of grain yielded no more than three or four new seeds.

Copenhagen might have had about 6000 inhabitants, a little bigger than Stockholm in Sweden and Bergen i Norway. Next in size came Flensborg in the province of Slesvig and Ribe in SW-Jutland. Other towns numbered less than 2,500 people.

The growing wealth was unevenly distributed. All over Europe a "feudal reaction" set in, reaching Denmark with the departure of Erik of Pomerania in 1438. The majority of farmers were now leaseholders, but heavy taxes on the freeholders left these not much better off.

In Slesvig serfdom leapt over the frontier from Germany, introduced by the Holstein lords on their estates. The peasants of the kingdom were never reduced to this low state, but in Zealand the lords introduced the obligation for a leaseholder's son to take over his father's farm, the leaseholder being the lords' labourer too. Otherwise he might run away to a town or take over a desolate farm in Jutland on easier terms. From this time the aristocrats began styling themselves as "free" and the rest of the people as "unfree". Originally "free" meant free of taxes, but it soon came to connote free in other respects as well.

The polarization of society was also clearly seen within the Church. With few exceptions all the bishops were of noble birth, and they took full possession of the parish churches, reducing the priests to episcopal servants.

Much of the bishops' wealth was invested in the churches. The old Romanesque buildings had their flat wooden ceilings replaced by Gothic vaults in brick, chancels were enlarged to provide room for the growing number of priests and choir boys, and towers, porches and chapels were added.

A very fine chancel is that of the cathedral of Haderslev in SE-Jutland, and c. 1450-1500 the cathedral of Aarhus was enlarged to become the biggest church in Denmark (300 feet long and 80 feet high). It has also the richest preserved catholic inventory, including murals. Its altarpiece from about 1470 was executed by Bernt Notke from Lübeck, the first artist whose name we know. It reflects that Lübeck was not only the leading commercial centre in the Baltic region, but also the cultural leader.

Whereas Denmark has practically no stained glass windows (one reason may be that they obscure light in the dark northern winters), hundreds of churches display murals from the Late Middle Ages, i.e. the last century of catholicism. A few of them are of high international artistic standard, the majority no doubt were executed by local workshops. They illustrate in a very lively fashion the stories of the Bible as well as the lives of the martyrs, but also reflect everyday life, showing clothing, handicrafts, etc. of the time.

The monasteries and convents were efficiently run as estates, supervised by the bishops. Few other than nobles became monks and nuns as the entry of payment was a leaseholder's farm. Theology was an exclusive study quite separate from the people. Even the mendicant orders, placed in the towns, and whose members should be beggars, began to accumulate property, but they still did a lot of good work among the lower classes. The two best preserved cloisters are the Carmelite monastery of Elsinore with its beautiful church of St. Mary, and the Dominican one of St. Catherine at Ribe.

Of all plagues no one was more feared than leprosy. As soon as somebody was found to have this disease, he or she was conducted out of the town to live at an institution of St. George (in Danish "St. Jørgen"). He was known to fight against evils, and this policy of isolation was successful. By the end of the Middle Ages Denmark was probably the first European country to have rid itself of this problem.

The Ascent of the Oldenburg Dynasty

In 1448 the crown was given to *Christian I*, a 22-year-old count of Oldenburg (near Bremen) for two reasons: he was the heir of the childless count of Holstein, which might open up for a future reunification of Denmark and Slesvig, and secondly he was willing to marry Dorothea, Christoffer's 18-year-old widow, who might otherwise have encumbered the state budget into a distant future.

The Oldenburg dynasty came to rule Denmark until 1863. Christian I also became king of Norway, but in Sweden fights between a national and a unionist party broke out.

Christian I liked grandeur, and with great ceremony he instituted the knighthood of the Order of the Elephant, but in financial matters he was completely irresponsible. However, when his uncle, the count of Holstein, died he squeezed every penny out of the situation. The knights of Holstein granted him large sums of money to prevent the reunification of Denmark and Slesvig and a consequent splitting of Slesvig and Holstein. The solution was reached at Ribe in 1460:– the king of Denmark was made count of Holstein by promising that Slesvig and Holstein were never to be separated. Christian considered this a great victory, but it meant that the still mainly Danish province of Slesvig remained under the German Holstein.

In the 1460s a privateering war with English ships developed over the rights of trade on Iceland. To secure Scottish aid Christian married off his daughter to King James III of Scotland. Not having any money for a dowry he handed over the Orkney and Shetland Islands instead in 1469.

In 1468 Christian I adopted a foreign idea of calling in a States-General with representation not only of the aristocracy and the clergy, but also of the citizens (i.e. the town dwellers) and the peasants. The meeting was held at Kalundborg, and here he promised to apply the habeas corpus act also to the lower classes to curb the abuses of the aristocracy. In return they voted large grants to the king, which he highly needed.

In 1474 Christian made a grand tour of Europe with great pomp. The German emperor raised the county of Holstein to a duchy, and in Rome the pope, who was given presents of smoked herring, gave him the right to erect a university. The nationalists in Sweden, in power after a Danish defeat in 1471, took action immediately and founded the university of Uppsala in 1477 to prevent Swedish clerical and civil servants from being instructed in Denmark, before the university of Copenhagen was instituted in 1479.

Christian's European Tour was financed through letters of credit. In 1480, one year before he died, his queen, Dorothea, was asked to countersign his letters of credit as she was more trustworthy than he was.

King Hans (1481-1513) in contrast to his father, Christian I, was not given to display. He was more like a merchant or even a huckster. Within ten years he had paid off all his father's debts, which made him very independent of grants by the council. His growing administration, correspondence and accounts allow us for the first time a good insight into a king's daily life.

He had to spend a lot of time travelling to inspect his kingdom, to settle disputes, and especially with his court to consume the taxes that were mainly paid in kind to the local governors. He often preferred a coach to horseback as he grew quite corpulent over the years. The coaches were without any kind of suspension, but well provided with cushions. But as much of his work as possible was done in writing from his beloved castle of Copenhagen. Here he enjoyed inviting friends, whether aristocrats or bourgeois, to his bath-house, where cold water was poured on hot stones in the old Scandinavian way. Afterwards they enjoyed a hearty Danish meal with beer followed by dice or card games.

In reality King Hans was a very shrewd person, and nobody ever came to understand his mind, least of all perhaps his queen Christine, who was very devoted to religion. She eventually took up residence at Odense, where she patronized a German artist, Claus Berg, whose workshop furnished churches in Funen with some of the finest altarpieces we have from the Catholic time, especially that of the cathedral of Odense.

The towns, however small, prospered under King Hans, who did much to improve their privileges. Most of the foreign trade was still in the hands of the Hanseatics, but he favoured the guilds of the local merchants and of the artisans, which offered a social security to the members. He also encouraged the erection of good town hospitals under the Order of the Holy Ghost, several of which are still preserved, such as those in Copenhagen and Randers (in E. Jutland).

In 1482 a book printer came to Odense and printed the first book in Denmark, in Latin. The first book in Danish was printed in Copenhagen in 1495. It was a versified chronicle of the history of the Danish kings. A decade later a collection of Danish proverbs followed, and both became bestsellers.

Hans managed to get some bishops who were not of noble birth installed, first of all Birger Gunnarsen as archbishop at Lund, the last great Catholic prelate in Denmark. As the bishops were automatically members of the state council, this caused a strife, which Hans did nothing to stop. It ended up with the murder of the aristocratic leader in 1502, after which Hans confiscated his estates. The aristocrats were divided. One of them, a sworn friend of the king, was allowed to erect the impressive stone castle of Glimmingehus in SE. Scania at this time. To a possible peasant army it was impregnable, but with the increased use of cannons, it constitued no danger to the royal power.

Hans had greater problems to attend to. In 1490 his much younger brother Frederik came of age and expected a dukedom. But as Denmark was indivisible, and Slesvig and Holstein were never more to be separated, the result was that they both obtained the title of "Duke of Slesvig and Holstein", and split the two provinces up in such a way that they both got parts of either. This was in accordance with the patch-work pattern of Germany, but as Slesvig remained the administrative centre, the German language continued to prevail. A consequence was also that Frederik came to nourish a hatred of his brother and of Denmark, feeling that he had been cheated.

Unlike his father Hans refrained from the use of privateering in his foreign policy. After having imposed an import duty on German beer he renewed the old rights of the Hanseatics of wholesaling in Danish towns to their pleasant surprise until the following year they learned that he had extended the rights of the English and Dutch skippers to include retail trade. In reality there were so few of the latter who sailed around Jutland that it changed little, but the aim of making Denmark less dependent on the Hanseatics was clear, and made Lübeck very suspicious.

Hans' greatest problem was Sweden where the nationalists had pre-vented him from becoming king. Now Hans made a treaty with the Grand Duke Ivan III of Moscow who made some futile raids on the bor-derland of Swedish-occupied Finland. This caused the unionists in Swe-den to start a civil war, and then Hans decided to take Sweden by power. He supplemented the armoured knights with a German mercenary army, called "lansquenets", for the first time in Scandinavia. The Swedish pea-sants were crushed whereas the aristocrats cleverly surrendered their castles without much fighting to their "lawful king", who was then crowned in Stockholm in 1497.

After that King Hans was at the peak of his power. He had attained even more than Margrethe, who had never reached a settlement at the southern frontier. But this did not last for long.

On the west coast of Holstein there was a small peasant republic of Ditmarsh, whose autonomy had for centuries been a thorn in the flesh of the counts of Holstein. The Ditmarshers in many ways resembled the semi-independent Frisians living to the north along the west coast of Sles-vig, and like those they obtained heavy crops of grass and grain, and entertained a considerable export of cattle to Hamburg, Bremen and the Netherlands. After some skirmishes the two rival brothers, King Hans and Duke Frederik, decided to incorporate Ditmarsh, one not begrudg-ing the other the profit. In the winter of 1500 an army of 10,000 men occupied the area of less than 500 sq. miles, until one rainy day when the thaw had set in, the Ditmarshers opened the sluices. The cannons sank into the mud, and armoured knights were drowned in the ditches.

This complete defeat started a chain reaction. First Sweden rioted, and a Danish blockade of the Swedish ports led to a war with Lübeck. To meet this situation King Hans founded shipyards to create a national navy, an idea which was new in Europe at that time. This proved a decisive action. Lübeck offered peace on condition that Denmark would limit the num-ber of Dutch ships entering the Baltic, but Hans declared that the Danish straits were open to all nations, which Lübeck had to accept in 1511. This marked the beginning of the decline of the Hanseatic monopoly of Baltic trade. At the same time the discovery of America shifted the focus of European trade westward.

When Hans died in 1513 the situation was still unsettled in Sweden.

King Hans was succeeded by his son, *Christian II* (1513-23), born in 1481. As a boy he had been very unruly, climbing roof-tops and spires, and for a while left to be brought up in the home of a Copenhagen mayor. As time went by his bourgeois outlook turned into a deep hatred of the aristocracy.

In 1506 his father had sent him to Norway to suppress opposition to heavy war taxation. On a military raid into Sweden he had destroyed castles, but forbidden his soldiers to infringe on the peasants' homes. He took up residence in the international trading city of Bergen, where he fell in love with a young girl, Dyveke ("Little Dove"), whose mother Sigbrit, a Dutch tradeswoman, soon became his financial adviser.

Before his coronation in 1513 Christian II was forced by the state council to sign the strictest coronation charter so far in Denmark – all the high administrative posts were to be reserved for aristocrats, and their judicial rights of the leaseholders were tightened, etc. One paragraph came to have special importance. It recognized the right of rebellion in case the king acted against the will of the council.

Christian wooed Isabella (in Danish Elisabeth), a young Hapsburg princess from Mechelen in the Low Countries, sister of the later emperor Charles V. The answer was affirmative on two conditions: he had to abandon his mistress (Dyveke) and his beard. They married in 1515, but Christian retained both Dyveke and his beard, and in return he only received a small part of the promised magnificent dowry of 250,000 guilders.

In 1518 Dyveke suddenly died, perhaps poisoned. Christian vented his rage on one of the leading aristocrats, Torben Oxe, who was executed, the exact charges being unknown. Christian's and Elisabeth's marriage turned out to be extremely harmonious, and even before Dyveke's death Elisabeth had established friendly relations with "Mother Sigbrit", who was detested by the aristocrats.

However, Christian soon gave the aristocrats a chance of gaining honour on the battlefield. In Sweden the leader of the unionists, the archbishop of Uppsala, had been imprisoned by the nationalists, and forced to resign, which gave Christian the opportunity of warfare. In 1520 his army conquered Stockholm, where he was crowned king of Sweden, and proclaimed a general amnesty. But the reinstituted archbishop wanted revenge and charged the Swedish aristocrats with heresy because they had interfered in church affairs. The result was the terrible "Bloodbath of Stockholm". Christian, declaring the amnesty invalid in matters of heresy, had some 80 noblemen, including two bishops, beheaded in the Grand Square. In Swedish history Christian is justly known as "Christian the Tyrant".

Nevertheless, other sides of his complex mind and work should also be considered. No doubt inspired by Sigbrit, who was in reality a very efficient minister of finance, he invited 200 peasants from the Netherlands to settle in the low and fertile island of Amager on the south of Copenhagen to improve the growing of vegetables. The present-day residents still retain many Dutch customs for example the "Beating the Barrel" festival in early February. Late in the nights Christian was editing a comprehensive set of laws far ahead of his time, including standardized weights and measures, a postal service, removal of town refuse, protection of shipwrecked seamen, qualification of school teachers, abolishment of harsh punishments, etc., and last but not least a much more just judicial system.

In the midst of this work he found time for a visit to the Netherlands, whose growing towns were his ideal. Here he had talks with Erasmus of Rotterdam, and was portrayed by Albrecht Dürer, showing his great interest in philosophy and arts. He was one of the first persons in Denmark to have his portrait painted in oil.

Nobody could mistake the king's intention of making the citizens the leading class of society, excluding the Hanseatics, radically reducing the power of the aristocracy, and creating a national church. But his laws never came into force.

It is no wonder that a chain reaction to put an end to all this started in Sweden. A young Swedish nobleman, Gustav Vasa, escaped from detention in Denmark, and became the leader of a Swedish war of independence. In 1523 he was crowned king of Sweden in Stockholm, which meant that the Nordic union no longer existed.

In this war Lübeck assisted the Swedes, and now the great lords of Jutland withdrew their allegiance from Christian, and offered his throne to his uncle, Duke Frederik of Slesvig and Holstein. Christian could count on the citizens and the peasants, but he probably doubted the loyalty of the noble lords of his castles. He conceived a plan of going to the Netherlands, having Elisabeth's dowry paid out and returning to Denmark heading an army of lansquenets to put a final end to aristocratic rule. He left Copenhagen on a ship with Elisabeth and Sigbrit in April, 1523, but unfortunately Charles V had enough problems himself, mainly caused by the riots and chaos following in the footsteps of Luther's activities.

In the meanwhile Frederik marched into Jutland and was proclaimed king *Frederik I* at Viborg. Ships from Lübeck carried his mercenary army to the islands, and after a siege of Copenhagen and Malmø, Denmark was back to aristocratic rule and Hanseatic monopoly of trade. Heavy taxes were levied on the peasants to pay for the war expenses, and life-long leaseholding was introduced.

Frederik I was thoroughly German and aristocratic. He retained his residence at the castle of Gottorp outside the town of Slesvig, leaving the government of Denmark in the hands of the council. This resulted in a vigorous suppression of the peasants.

In his coronation charter Frederik I had promised to uphold the Roman Catholic Church, but like most of the North German princes he had an eye on the Church's properties. His oldest son, Christian, had personally attended Luther's plea at Worms in 1521, and had become a convinced and declared Lutheran. His father let him rule the northern parts of Slesvig, and here, at Haderslev, he carried through the reformation of the Church in the late 1520s.

The real reformer of the Danish Church was a monk, Hans Tavsen, who after a visit to Luther's Wittenberg, began preaching the new ideas first at Viborg and later in Copenhagen under the protection of the king. Like Luther he married, and encouraged people to sing hymns in their own language. In the strife between the Lutherans and the "Papists" many means were used, first of all printed pamphlets, but also wall paintings as is seen in the village church of Brøns in SW. Jutland.

The first victims of the new movement were the mendicant monasteries in the towns, whose inhabitants were in some cases chased out by the citizens, instigated by Mogens Goye, the richest aristocrat and leading member of the council. None of the aristocratic monasteries and convents in the rural districts were touched, and there were no cases of fanatic brutality.

Christian II in his humble exile at Lier near Antwerp was also influenced by Luther, whom he visited. He invited a Danish author, Christian Pedersen, to live with him. He had formerly published the first Latin-Danish dictionary and Saxo's History of Denmark, thus preserving this for posterity (the copy which Shakespeare later used, see page 22). Now he translated the New Testament into Danish, copies of which were in great numbers smuggled into Denmark. There was nothing the Catholic Church feared more than the translation of the Bible from the holy Latin into the "vulgar" languages.

But Christian II depended on Charles V, who was the great defender of the Catholic cause, and swore allegiance to the old Church. In 1530 he received an installment of his queen's dowry, although she had died two years earlier. For this money he equipped a fleet and sailed to Norway, where he was proclaimed king in 1531. From Copenhagen ships arrived with envoys from Frederik I and the council, promising Christian safe-conduct to talks with his uncle. Christian embarked with only a few at-tendants, but the ships passed Copenhagen and continued to the Castle of Sønderborg in S. Jutland, where he was imprisoned.

Shortly after this, in 1533, king Frederik I died. The bishops and the majority of the aristocrats refused to elect his eldest son Christian as suc-cessor because of his Lutheran convictions, and put off the election, which meant that Denmark was in reality an aristocratic republic.

The citizens and the peasants were furious. They wanted to reinstall the imprisoned Christian II, and for this they were now offered help from a most unexpected side. In Lübeck a revolution against the oligarchy had taken place, and the new mayor promised his colleagues of Copenhagen and Malmø money and ships to overthrow the aristocratic council, which had refused to prevent Dutch ships from entering the Baltic. This was a desperate act as the Hanseatics had good cause to fear Christian II more than any other ruler. However, a professional German army was hired, led by a distant relative of the Danish royal house, count Christof-fer of Oldenburg, and a new civil war was begun. Later aristocratic writers called it "The Count's Feud" to obscure the fact that this, the last civil war in Denmark, ended up as a social clash of unheard-of-dimen-sions in which everyone had to choose side. The hatred and brutality that had been absent in the religious strife now exploded.

In the beginning, in 1534, however, the count's army occupied most of Zealand and Scania without much fighting. The count was received as a liberator by the people, and most of the aristocratic governors of the castles renewed loyalty to Christian II. The savagery started in Funen where the aristocrats took up the fighting. The bishop's castles were burnt down by the people, and the mercenaries of the aristocracy ravaged the towns before withdrawing to Holstein.

In Jutland Mogens Goye, the leader of the Lutheran minority of the aristocrats, called for at meeting on July 4, 1534, where he convinced the other lords that it was urgent to elect Frederik I's eldest son as *King Chri-stian III*. The oldest of the bishops and the only one to be respected as a true Catholic burst out weeping. He knew this meant the end of the Catholic Church in Denmark.

Christian having waited patiently at Slesvig immediately hired a mercenary force under general Rantzau, who first blockaded Lübeck, and then marched into Jutland, where a riot had spread from the north. Christian II's admiral, known as "skipper Clement" had landed in his native town of Aalborg from where he had led a revolutionary march of citizens and peasants towards Sønderborg to liberate the imprisoned Christian II. Everywhere aristocratic strongholds were set on fire, but facing the advancing professional army Clement's followers fled, to be finally crushed at Aalborg, where the city was exposed to a bloody orgy. Freeholders who could not prove that they had not taken part in the riot were reduced to leaseholders (reversed burden of proof).

In 1535 Rantzau conquered Funen whose towns were once more ravaged. Now King Gustav Vasa of Sweden, who had good reasons to hate Christian II joined the war by sending an army into Scania and providing ships to carry Rantzau's army over to Zealand.

The final defeat of the revolutionaries came in 1536. Lübeck withdrew from the war early enough to obtain some advantage – the taxes from the island of Bornholm for 50 years. In April Malmø surrendered, whereas the besieged Copenhagen held out as long as it could get supplies from the small island of Amager. After its loss the city was starved and surrendered on July 29. The chief mayor in whose father's house Christian II had also been brought up, committed suicide.

Reformation, Renaissance and Aristocratic Rule

1536 – 1660

Now Christian III was finally king of the entire kingdom, and as long as the 12,000 professional soldiers were still at hand he was politically very strong. But the country was devastated, and the economic situation was desperate. The debt of the state amounted to more than 13 times of the normal revenue of one year. In the first case this had been laid out by the rich Holstein knighthood, which was the great victor, having put its man on the Danish throne, but Christian III was a complete contrast to his self-contained father, very out-spoken and with a much broader world view. Shocked by the cruelty of the war, from now on he always tried to obtain peaceful settlements, internally as well as externally. He did declare that the lower classes had behaved like mad dogs, but gave a general amnesty – with one exception – within a week after his entry into Copenhagen he had all the bishops captured, blaming the war on them because they had prevented the election of a king in 1533. In his own words, "The loyalty they owed the country a fly had probably carried away on its rump." (Most of them willingly transferred their loyalty from the pope to the king, and obtained posts as local governors, etc.)

This was in reality a coup d'etat. The Catholic Church, possessing one-third of all land in Denmark, was to pay for the war expenses. The king's share of the country rose from one-sixth to almost half though the aristocracy had a fair deal too, and now owned about 40% of the land. The number of freeholders was probably halved as a result of the war to about 7% of the peasants. A serious problem was the great number of beggars who constituted perhaps 15% of the population, many of whom were no doubt peasants who never dared to return to their homes after their participation in the riot.

In a States-General held in Copenhagen in October, 1536, where nobles, citizens and peasants were present, but no clerics, as the Lutheran clergy was to be strictly spiritual, the official Reformation of the Church was confirmed.

Now the king was the head of the Church, the tithes went to the state, and the church ministers became civil servants. There was to be no archbishop, but in reality the bishop of Zealand took his place. Hans Tavsen became the instructor of Lutheran parsons, but most of the parish priests remained in office. The aristocratic monasteries and convents were allowed to continue their Catholic practices, but not to take in novices. Christian III's modesty was also seen from the fact that Christian Pedersen, Christian II's sworn ally, was asked to translate the entire Bible, which was printed in 1550. By doing so he became "the father of written Danish", as his Bible became the standard reference for future authors.

The new Church was in no way more tolerant than the old one. Only Lutheran churches were allowed, and the three professors of theology were to censor what was to be printed. In the Catholic countries heretics were burnt, while in the Protestant world the burning of witches spread. Torture that had been so abundantly used in the civil war had come to stay.

Now a slow process to change the church interiors began. Pulpits and pews were installed, and baptismal fonts were moved to the chancels as baptism was now a sacrament. New epitaphs of nobles took the place of catholic side-altars and saints. The change to protestantism was no blessing for the poor. As good deeds played a lesser role than before, donations dwindled, and hospitals and schools became a burden on town budgets.

In this time of upheaval when the old picture of the world collapsed due to discoveries and inventions new problems arose. A scourge to replace leprosy was venereal disease, which caused the closing of public bath-houses because they had also been places of various forms of "entertainment". This meant that personal hygiene decreased and that epidemics became constantly recurring. Another problem was strong liquor, the distilling of which spread rapidly and constituted a special danger to young persons.

The remaining part of the century (1536-1600) became the great epoch of aristocracy in which time more than 1,500 manor-houses were erected. In the beginning they were strongholds to resist peasant assaults, but as time went by moats, drawbridges, spires, etc., became more a matter of prestige and convention.

Johan Friis, who as a young nobleman had become chancellor under Frederik I, became the leading statesman. Retained by the rebels, he was so much respected that they allowed him to go to Luther's town of Wittenberg to study, but just at the right time before the conclusion of the civil war he was back as Christian III's chancellor. The two had much in common. As an aristocrat Johan Friis belonged to the moderates, and though he shunned confrontation, he had to rebuke his equals several times for blatant abuses of peasants. But generally there was no limit to the work the leaseholders had to do for their lords. The big estates were mainly run by the peasants' labour. A leaseholder had to have just as many horses as cows because of his work on the large estate fields, while his wife and daughters served in the kitchens and laundries of the manors.

Many of the new manor-houses had their bases made of granite stones from the superfluous Catholic churches that were torn down, and the peasants dug out moats, transported stones and baked bricks with their blood, sweat and tears.

Johan Friis erected two of the most characteristic early manor-houses, Hesselager in Funen and Borreby in SW. Zealand. In Funen too, the marshall of the army built Egeskov on oakpiles in a lake in the 1550s. Besides Funen and S. Zealand there is a great concentration of these small castles in the islands of Lolland and Falster as well as in Scania and Djursland of E. Jutland, i.e. where much of the richest soil of the country is to be found.

In Slesvig and Holstein the intricate territorial division was renewed, now between the king and his brother Adolf, whose ducal line, named "the Gottorps" after their residential castle at Slesvig, was to cause Denmark endless trouble in times to come.

Christian III rebuilt and reinforced some of the old castles such as Nyborg and Malmø, but personally he lived very humbly, much to the annoyance of his queen, Dorothea. In 1549 he reached a settlement with his cousin, Christian II, who renounced all claims on the throne, after which he obtained residence at the castle of Kalundborg where he spent the time hunting and fishing. The castle of Sønderborg, where he had been imprisoned, was taken over by Dorothea who rebuilt it. Her chapel there is our oldest existing Lutheran chapel in Denmark.

The two cousins, king Christian III and ex-king Christian II both died within the first three weeks of 1559. Christian III received a magnificent sarcophagus in the cathedral of Roskilde, while Christian II was humbly interred at Odense.

When Christian III died in 1559 most of the national debt had been repaid. His eldest son, *Frederik II*, now 25, became a truly aristocratic king, preferring tournaments, hunting and drinking to boring administrative work.

No sooner had the peaceful king died than duke Adolf and the Holstein knights prepared a new war on the independent peasants of Ditmarsh to revenge the defeat in 1500. Frederik II adopted the idea, but the council vetoed it. However, it had no rights in Slesvig and Holstein, so the king and his uncle carried it through by their authority as dukes. Taught by experience they chose the summer (of 1559) for the expedition, and were victorious. After the bloody conquest the old general Rantzau prevented a massacre, and the Ditmarshers retained local self-government.

In 1560 Frederik II issued a maritime law to protect ships and seamen against piracy and violation in case of wreck. It also prescribed lights of burning pitch to guide ships around the Skaw (the northernmost tip of Jutland) and through the Kattegat and the Sound. This was a demand of the Netherlands in return for the payment of the Sound Toll. At this time 60% of the ships passing the Sound were Dutch. In contrast to the exclusive Hanseatics the Dutch depended largely on local merchants which gave room for increased Danish trade and shipping.

The possession of the island of Gotland was important for the Danish dominance of the Baltic Sea, but caused many skirmishes with Sweden. However, Christian III and Gustav Vasa had always managed to find peaceful solutions. In 1560 Erik XIV succeeded his father in Sweden, and with two young hotspurs on the thrones and a new generation of noblemen who had no memory of the wars of their fathers war was inevitable. The old Johan Friis vainly voted against the war. This war started in 1563 and lasted for seven years, devastated the border regions of Denmark, Norway and Sweden and settled nothing.

One of the many who fell in the war was the Danish admiral, Herluf Trolle, who bequethed his estate of Herlufsholm, a former monastery near Næstved in S. Zealand, for the establishment of a school, mainly for the sons of noblemen. His relatives were furious, but after a long process his beloved widow, Birgitte Goye (a daughter of Mogens Goye, see page 42) realized the plan, creating our oldest Public School in the British sense of the word. Birgitte Goye was the most outstanding of many

Painting dated 1561, in the National Museum, showing the new Protestant church service with sermon, baptism, and communion "in both kinds". (p. 46).

The Rosenholm Castle or Manor House, E. Jutland, erected by the Rosenkranz family 1565-1625. Its location in a low watery area is characterstic. (p. 50).

The Castle of Kronborg at Elsinore strategically situated on the NE. tip of Zealand, where the Sound, the main waterway to the Baltic, is only a few miles wide. (p. 33, 50, 60).

The Frederiksborg Castle in N. Zealand, named after Fr. II, but built by Chr. IV 1600-20. The big tower in front is the gate-tower. (p. 49, 54, 103).

learned noblewomen of the time. It is mainly due to them that so many old ballads were preserved. As a young girl Birgitte Goye had refused to marry the nobleman her father had chosen for her. The matter ended up in the state council which finally took her side. This is the first known case of that kind. In her home she tutored noble girls.

Birgitte Goye's sister was married to a brother of Torben Oxe who had been executed by Christian II in 1517. Her son, Peder Oxe, became the leading statesman after Johan Friis. Peder Oxe was liked by few, but he had one of the greatest capacities for law and economics ever produced by Denmark. After studies abroad he returned to Denmark at the age of 17, now the head of this prominent family. Through series of lawsuits against relatives and neighbours he gained control of ever increasing lands until Frederik II in 1558 asked Herluf Trolle to prosecute him on behalf of the crown. Having the fate of his uncle in his mind he left the country to join the court of Christian II's daughter, Christine, Duchess of Lorraine, who was constantly intriguing against Denmark.

In 1566 the financial situation of Denmark, due to the war, was so hopeless that the council forced Frederik II to call back Peder Oxe, his worst personal enemy. Until his death in 1575 Oxe was the real leader of the country. The king hardly ever appeared in Copenhagen, and spent most of his time in N. Zealand building the first Frederiksborg Castle and hunting in the nearby forests.

Oxe took advantage of the fact that the Netherlands were struggling their fight for freedom against the Spaniards to raise the Sound Toll by 50%. This made it possible to continue the war with Sweden until a peace was reached in 1570 at an international conference, which decided that Denmark was to retain Gotland. In reality, however, none of the points of disagreement were solved.

As a matter of curiosity it may be mentioned that the Earl of Bothwell, former husband of Mary Stuart of Scotland, fled to Norway in 1567. He died in the castle of Dragsholm in NW. Zealand, where he was held prisoner, probably in the hope of a ransom. His tomb can be seen in the local village church of Faarevejle.

Denmark recovered remarkbly quickly after the war because Europe was experiencing an economic boom, especially due to the cargoes of silver from South America. The fast growing cities in Western Europe demanded ever increasing quantities of farm produce from the Baltic region, including Denmark. The situation of the peasants eased a little, but they paid their dues in labour and produce and had few superfluous goods with which to obtain advantages from the rising prices. The profits went almost entirely to the aristocratic lords who were now so busy that they had to have assistance from the merchants for their export. In this way the towns obtained a share of the increased wealth, too.

Many lords began to erect four-winged manor-houses, but most of them were never completed. One of the exceptions is Rosenholm, the family seat of the Rosenkrantzes, near Aarhus in E. Jutland, built 1565-1625. Other impressive castles from this period are Vallø in E. Zealand, erected by Peder Oxe's widow, Mette Rosenkrantz at 1585, and Voergaard in N. Jutland from about 1590.

From the steadily increasing revenues from the Sound Toll Frederik II began rebuilding the 150-year-old castle at Elsinore, for which he mainly employed architects and artist from the Netherlands, many of whom were refugees from Antwerp which was reconquered and recatholicized by the Spaniards. The castle ended up as the most outstanding renaissance building in Denmark, and Frederik II gave it the name of Kronborg (i.e. "The Castle of the Crown"). It is extremely doubtful whether Shakespeare ever visited it though an English troupe of actors gave a performance here in 1585, when the castle was inaugurated, but from them or any English seaman who had sailed into the Baltic he would be familiar with this "Danish Gibraltar".

The relations between Frederik II's Denmark and Elizabeth's England were strained when the English "Moscovy Company" began to sail north of Norway to Archangelsk, thus evading the Sound Toll. Finally England acknowledged "the strait" (sic) between Norway and Greenland as Danish waters, and agreed to pay a symbolic fee. After this Frederik II received the English Order of the Garter, probably the one preserved in the Rosenborg Castle.

The prosperity of the time was also reflected in the Danish churches where the great majority of altar-pieces and pulpits date from 1570-1640, in style developing from the pure renaissance to the much more voluminous and ornate early baroque. Epitaphs of nobles threatened to fill up the churches until Frederik II forbid them – in reality to prevent Peder Oxe's widow from making a large monument in Our Lady's Church in Copenhagen (which was not officially a cathedral, the bishop's official residence being still at Roskilde).

The greatest theologian under Frederik II was Niels Hemmingsen, who was very liberal and open to criticism of Luther's dogmas. He doubted the existence of witches, or at least he declared himself convinced that they could not fly, but when he approached the Calvinist conception of communion as a symbolic act and not one of actual transformation of bread and wine into Christ's flesh and blood, the alarm bells began to ring throughout the Lutheran world. Orthodox Germans called him a "crypto-Calvinist" and a heretic, and due to pressure mainly from the court of Saxony, the government found a truly Danish solution – he was dismissed from his professorship at the University of Copenhagen, but secured a livelihood as a teacher at the cathedral of Roskilde. Nevertheless the effect was that Protestant enthusiasm, evident in hundreds of hymns, etc., dried up in the Lutheran orthodoxy after 1600.

Of even greater international renown was the astronomer Tycho Brahe (1546-1601) who was born into an ancient noble family of Scania. An eclipse of the sun turned his interest to astronomy and astrology. A treatise on a new star "De nova stella" brought him fame. From his observatory in the island of Hveen in the Sound he carried out the most exact observations of celestial bodies ever made in the West. But he was a highly controversial person. He lived together with a non-aristocratic woman, he refused to believe in the Devil, tyrannized the peasants, and as a governor he neglected his duties, e.g. to see to it that the lights for the shipping were burning on dark nights. In 1597 there was a rift between him and the young king Christian IV, after which he went to Prague where Kepler became his assistant before he died in 1601. Some years later Kepler published "The Laws of the Universe" based on Brahe's observations, drawing the conclusion that Brahe had not reached, that the sun, not the earth, was the centre of our system.

Frederik II died in 1588 at the age of 54. The official Danish historian said in his necrology that if he could have refrained from drinking, he might have lived for many a day.

At this time his oldest son, *Christian IV*, was only eleven (born in 1577). Until his coronation in 1596 the state council ruled in a remarkably loyal way, none of the councillors taking personal advantage of the situation. This was the last generation of great aristocratic personalities. One of the councillors who no doubt inspired Christian IV in his future work was Christoffer Valkendorf who reorganized the administration of Copenhagen, improved its ramparts and habour, gave the city its first regular water supply, transported through 4 miles of hollowed-out tree trunks, furnished some of its churches with towers and founded a student dormitory. Another was the chancellor of justice, Arild Huitfeldt, who carried through what so many learned historians had never achieved, writing a Danish history from Saxo (about 1180, see page 21) to his own time. This was intended to be a history book for Christian IV, and remained the standard history of Denmark until Holberg's, written in the 1730s.

In 1589 Christian IV's elder sister Ann was to marry James VI of Scotland, but her fleet was blown back to Norway by a contrary gale. This occasioned the burning of many witches in Denmark. Impatient for his bride James now arrived in person, married Ann, and visited Brahe in Hveen and Hemmingsen at Roskilde. Unfortunately no reports tell us if this great witch-hunter, called the wisest fool of Christendom, discussed devils and witches with the two rationalists.

Christian IV received a thorough theoretic and physical training at Sorø in Central Zealand, where his father had erected a "Knightly Academy" in the former monastic buildings. When the prince travelled with the court, his instructors followed. According to tradition he was taught navigation on the lake by the castle of Skanderborg in E. Jutland, and the news of his father's death reached him at Kronborg.

In 1595, impatient to be crowned, he undertook a journey to Protestant courts in Germany, where an especially splendid reception awaited him at Berlin, the capital of the growing princedom of Brandenburg (later Prussia).

At the age of 19, in 1596, he was crowned in Copenhagen at the most magnificent festival ever held in Denmark. A new crown full of symbolic figures fashioned according to his own ideas as well as a rich riding outfit with diamond and pearl embroidery (now in the Rosenborg Castle) had been made. The festivities which lasted for a month included tournaments, fireworks and sightseeing tours to Kronborg and Frederiksborg as well as heavy drinking. The horses of the invited visitors amounted to 3,000, and before the end of the festival Copenhagen was short of food and wine.

All this pomp was to show that Christian was one of the richest monarchs in Europe, mainly due to the fact that the Sound Toll was a royal prerogative, because though his two kingdoms of Denmark and Norway experienced prosperity, they were far less developed than the rest of Western Europe.

Shortly after his coronation he was married to Anna Kathrine of Brandenburg, and entered his first large building project, that of rebuilding the castle of Kolding at the border of Denmark and Slesvig.

Of all figures acting on the stage of Danish history, Christian IV is the one we seem to know best, not only because he was the most active of our kings, but especially because more than 3,000 of his personally written letters are preserved along with his diaries and many sketches, together with a multitude of portraits and personal belongings, including a nightshirt and slippers, not to mention the innumerable anecdotes told about him.

Most of his letters are very impulsive, full of good humour and irony, sometimes verging on arrogance, which manifested itself when he deprived Tycho Brahe of the island of Hveen (see above). Perhaps the most negative thing to be said about him is the fact that he seemed to leave no room for other personalities to unfold. No matter was too insignificant to escape his attention, but at the same time his great plans and political ideas were never lost from view.

From his earliest childhood his heart was set on the sea, and soon after his coronation he began a grand-scale rebuilding of the navy, on which the dominion of the Baltic Sea depended, and in 1598 he set out on a project of furnishing Copenhagen with a new naval habour. Three long piers projecting from the Castle Island were constructed, for which conscripted peasants delivered the materials. On the first pier the 520 feet long Arsenal was erected with solid brick walls, 11 feet thick (completed in 1604, and now a military museum), on the second a parallel building was built for the provisions of the ships, mainly consisting of flour, smoked pork, salted fish and dried peas (the basin between these two piers now contains the Royal Library Gardens), and on the third pier the eight-storey-high brewery was built (completed in 1618) as large quantities of beer were necessary because of the dry and salty nature of the food and the bad drinking water of the cities.

In Christian IV's foreign policy the growing power of Sweden played an important role. Sweden no longer split up by fractions now had an efficient government, and mines to exploit the newly detected large deposits of iron and copper had been opened up. After successful fights with the Russians, the Swedish dominance of Finland was extended to Estonia, and in Northern Scandinavia the Swedish king began taxing the nomadic Lapps.

To secure his rights Christian IV in 1599 undertook a very adventurous voyage of more than 1500 miles along the unchartered coast of Norway around the North Cape, and inspected the frontier between Norway and Russia. He formed a special interest in Norway so he often revisited the country.

In 1606 he paid a visit to his favourite sister Ann, whose husband James had suddenly become king of England after the death of Elizabeth in 1603. In and around London he saw everything worth seeing, studying not least the architecture of contemporary English castles. He was impressed by the size of the Westminster Abbey as well as by the activities of the Exchange of the City. In his diary he noted down the measurements of the cannons of the Tower of London, while in the evenings he had some jolly drinking-bouts with James.

After his return he was shocked to learn that the Swedish king had declared himself "King of the Lapps", and that the Swedish expansion southwards from Estonia had reached Riga, which was under the king of Poland. In 1611 he persuaded the reluctant council to declare war on Sweden, called "The Kalmar War" named after a Swedish frontier castle that Denmark conquered. The war lasted until 1613 when Sweden acknowledged Danish sovereignty of Lappland and agreed to pay war damages, but the outcome of the war was no doubt a great disappointment to Christian. The new young Swedish king Gustavus Adolphus had proved a potent danger to Denmark.

The first quarter of the 17th century became Christian IV's great building period. After he had initiated the works at Kolding and Copenhagen already mentioned, in 1601 he tore down his father's castle of Frederiksborg, situated on three islets in a lake in the heart of the royal hunting domain in N. Zealand, to have it replaced by a much more spectacular one. Here he was his own master-builder, signing contracts with the various artisans and personally scrutinizing all the accounts, but for the more difficult technical problems he no doubt depended on the assistance of two sons of his father's architect Steenwinckel from Antwerp. He also employed a great number of mainly Dutch artists to make fountains, sculptures, tapestries, etc. In the midst of the proceedings he changed his original plans, perhaps inspired by what he had seen in England – he enlarged the chapel and added a barbican (a gate tower), in both of which he anticipated the baroque style by almost half a century. The result was a much more festive-looking castle at the expense of regularity.

It was, however, his small summer castle of Rosenborg that became his most personal building, and the one he loved the most. This he could reach in about 20 minutes on horseback from his old-fashioned and overcrowded residential castle in Copenhagen, as he placed it just outside the ramparts of the city in a garden, still called "The King's Garden". Here indeed he played his own pragmatic architect, starting out with a plain house in 1606 and ending up in 1633 with a castle with towers, but the result of this piece-meal construction was nevertheless one of great uniformity in his own very personal variation of the Dutch renaissance style. Inside, the great art collector created in1611 one of the oldest preserved art galleries in Europe, the panels of which were contructed for 45 Dutch and Flemish paintings that he had acquired in the preceding years. He also played with all kinds of technical devices, such as speaking tubes in the walls, and drawbridges to be turned with a key, and in the garden he experimented with seeds and bulbs from Asia and America.

The Danish towns experienced a boom in the first half of Christian IV's reign. The population of Copenhagen reached about 25,000, and still to-day a great number of half-timbered merchants' houses bear witness to the building activities in such towns as Elsinore, Køge and Kalundborg in Zealand, and Aalborg and Randers in Jutland. Other examples of such houses have in our century been moved to the open-air museum of Aarhus, called "The Old Town".

The main exports were still grain and cattle whereas salted fish played a much lesser role than in the Catholic days. In good years half a million barrels of grain and 50,000 head of cattle were exported, the latter being walked most of the way along the old "Army Road" down through Jutland, and every year some 5000 ships, mainly Dutch, paid the Sound Toll at Elsinore.

Now eventually the peasants, too, got a share of the increasing wealth. Chimneys and stained glass windows became common even in farmhouses. These go together because the smoke hole was also a source of light. In a letter Christian IV wrote that he did not mind staying overnight in peasants' houses, but "not in smoke houses".

Christian IV was a true mercantile king who constantly intervened in matters of trade and manufacture, introducing high tariffs on certain imported goods to protect local production. He supported new commercial companies and the establishment of industial water mills, from which the Mill River north of Copenhagen received its name. The use of capital punishment was much reduced because criminals as well as vagrant orphans could serve in the workhouses he erected. The latter died like flies in spite of the fact that he personally saw to it that they had sufficient to eat and large quantities of beer to drink.

In this headlong attempt to develop Denmark industrially he was not very successful, but laid a foundation for later generations to build on. In his fight against the monopolies of the artisans' guilds he was almost completely defeated. In 1613 he simply forbade the guilds as they limited the number of masters. He made handicraft a free trade, not realizing the positive aspects of the guilds, e.g. that they guaranteed the quality of their work and constituted a social network for their members. The journeymen who were part of an international brotherhood began a boycott of Denmark which soon made the king retreat and allow the guilds again, but now to be supervised by the town authorities.

Envious of the profitable world trade of the Western European countries, in 1610 Christian sent out a Norwegian sea captain, Jens Munk, to find a North-East passage to India, but he became stuck in the ice north of Russia. So in 1618 he decided to follow the traditional route to East India, erecting the first Danish shareholding company to pay for an expedition round Africa, led by a 24-year-old nobleman, Ove Gedde. In spite of mutiny and epidemics on board this became relatively successful as the small fishing village of Tranquebar on the SE. coast of India was made a Danish trading point where pepper could be bought, spices being the main driving force for European discoveries.

In 1619 when Gedde was still on his way to India, Jens Munk was sent out to find a North-West passage from the newly discovered Hudson Bay to India. 62 of the 65 men died from scurvy in the winter at the mouth of the river, later named the Churchill River, at approximately the same latitude as Denmark, but with a much colder climate. In the following summer Munk with two other men managed to return to Norway on the smallest of the three ships, only to be rebuked of the loss of the two bigger ships by a bitter king who now realized that Denmark-Norway was never to be a centre of world trade because of its location.

In 1618, just having finished his naval harbour in Copenhagen with its three piers, Christian IV set out on the largest of all his projects, that of creating a good commercial harbour next to the naval one, and founding a new township to be called Christianshavn (i.e. "Christian's Port") across the channel of the harbour. On a fourth and longer pier a "Bourse" was built as a commodity exchange for the merchants and their imported goods. The building was crowned by an unusual spire made up of four dragons, and beautifully ornamented, perhaps because it was right outside Christian's windows of the castle. It was inaugurated in 1624, and a room in it was reserved for the postmaster-general, as a postal service was now organized with a weekly connection to Hamburg and Oslo. At the end of the pier a drawbridge was constructed on oak piles, which functioned for 250 years until 1868, across the channel to the is-

Prospect of Copenhagen 1611. The big building is the Castle. In the foreground Chr. IV's new naval harbour with the Arsenal to the left. (cf. p. 53).

Interior of the Arsenal (see above), now a military museum.

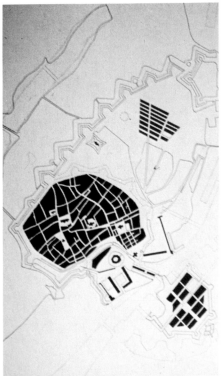

Christian IV supposedly instructing his chief engineer as to the new defence line around Copenhagen in the 1630s. In the background the Rosenborg Castle, where this small painting is to be seen (p. 60).

Map showing Christian IV's extensions of Copenhagen. The old city in black. On its south side his new harbour (p. 53) and across the channel the new township of Christianshavn on the shore of Amager (p. 56). Right outside the old city the Rosenborg Castle with "The King's Garden" and further the township of Nyboder (p. 60). The fact that the fortifications were unfinished caused the Danish defeat to Sweden in 1658 (p. 62-63).

land of Amager. Along the shore of this island the new township rose out of the water with houses built on piles. To-day these houses in Strandgade (i.e. "Strand or Beach Street") are among the oldest citizens' houses in Copenhagen. For the whole of the project the king once more depended on Dutch engineers.

As in all the ten towns Christian founded, the purpose of Christianshavn was both military and commercial. It was cut through by canals for barges and surrounded by a semi-circular rampart and moat so that Copenhagen's harbour was now protected from all sides and came to appear like a river. With this great project Christian had no doubt hoped to take a good share of the trade of Hamburg and Lübeck as the growing tension between Protestants and Catholics had a negative effect on the economic life of Germany, but in the same year he commenced the project, in 1618, the Thirty Years' War broke out, and immediately the Danish export and the Sound Toll began to dwindle.

However, until 1625 Christian IV continued founding new towns. In his part of the German province of Holstein, on the north bank of the Elb he founded the fortified town of Glückstadt ("City of Fortune"), which was to compete with Hamburg, but it lacked the hinterland, and has remained a small town with a central square from which streets radiate to the ramparts. All his other new towns were planned like checker boards such as Christianshavn as well as Christianstad which he founded on an island in a river in NE. Scania near the Swedish border, whose church is the biggest and the most beautiful of his church buildings.

In 1623 Norway's biggest town of Bergen with more than 10,000 inhabitants, was ravaged by a fire. Even before he had received the usual petition for financial aid, Christian sent a detailed plan of how the city had to be rebuilt. But on the limited area between its seven hills there was no room for his intended wide and straight streets which would also have been unbecoming to this international and liberal city, so it was rebuilt just as crowded as before and mainly in wood.

The following year Oslo suffered an even more devastating fire, and Christian resolutely moved the town a couple of miles to be placed immediately below the Akershus Castle, his main residence in Norway, which he had just started to rebuild. The new town received the name of Christiania (or Kristiania), but in 1924 it was renamed Oslo.

To a mercantile king metals played a central role. From Germany mine experts were called to Norway where they established a couple of iron mines. Although they were much smaller than the Swedish ones, it meant that from then on Norway furnished itself and Denmark with iron stoves for the next centuries. In 1623 an earthquake revealed a vein of silver in Norway. Christian ordered thanksgiving services to be held, and a mine called Kongsberg ("the King's Mountain") was established, but all together the profits of the mines were so trifling that in the meagre years to come they were turned into private enterprises.

The Great Turning Point of Danish History

Like all other religious wars the armed confrontation between the Protestant North and the Catholic South of Germany turned out to be of extreme fanaticism and cruelty. The riot of the Czech people in Bohemia which had prompted the war, was soon repressed by the Imperial League which after that began to occupy Protestant princedoms in Central Germany, everywhere chasing "heretics". Very soon it became obvious that the Protestants lacked a military leader. There were two candidates, the king of Denmark and the king of Sweden. Both Holland and England seemed willing to pay large sums for a war on the Catholic empire. But as Gustavus Adolphus of Sweden demanded prohibitive payment and large expeditionary forces, he excluded himself and renewed his war on Poland to get control of the south coast of the Baltic, after he had conquered Riga and taken control of the entire east coast of the Baltic.

In 1625 Christian IV accepted the leadership of the Protestant Union. As an idealist he wanted to be the champion of the Protestant cause, but his main drive was jealousy of Sweden's progress, and the hope of placing some of his sons as dukes in German princedoms, and thus take control of the mouths of the big German rivers for military and economic reasons.

From the moment Christian made the decision, everything began to go wrong for him. Within a few months his two best allies, James of England and Maurice of Holland died, and strong opposition to the plans appeared both in the Parliament in London and in the States-General in the Hague. The Danish council also proved strongly opposed to an open confrontation with the German emperor. But Christian IV had committed himself so much that he decided to enter the war as duke of Holstein with an army of 20,000 soldiers (of whom about 10% were Danish). In 1626 he suffered a terrible defeat at Lutter am Baremberg south of Brunswick. Personally Christian showed great bravery, but against the experienced imperial generals he had no chance. With a few hundred men he fled to Jutland which the imperial troops occupied in the following year, naturally not respecting the fictitious frontier between Holstein and Denmark. As the only fortress, Christian's new town of Glückstadt resisted, because Dutch ships provided it with food as the imperial plans of recatholicizing Jutland and excluding the Dutch from the Baltic became known in the Netherlands.

The Danish navy was able not only to prevent an occupation of the islands, but also to blockade some of the German ports. This was the situation when King Gustavus Adolphus of Sweden, having pacified Poland, entered the theatre of war as a new Protestant champion, in which role he was more successful than Christian. In 1629 Denmark was offered peace on relatively easy terms. No Danish territory had to be ceded, but the king had to call back his sons from German princedoms and to promise not to interfere in German matters.

So now after almost a hundred years of progress Denmark was suddenly impoverished, and the province of Jutland devastated. The consequence was political reaction and intolerance, people were encouraged to inform against persons who lived an "un-Christian life" to detract attention from the grumbling over heavy taxation. Townsfolk openly began to criticize the privileges of the nobility who had in great numbers fled Jutland instead of defending it. To this were added other calamities. In 1629 the Kronborg Castle of Elsinore was destroyed by a fire, and in 1634 the North Sea flooded the west coast of Slesvig, drowning about 8000 people and a much larger number of cattle. These floods often seem to have occurred at times when the population had suffered from wars and subsequent epidemics, and the maintenance of the dikes consequently was defective.

Christian IV also had numerous personal grievances. A few years after the death in 1612 of his first wife Queen Anna Kathrine, in which marriage there were six children, he married "to his left hand" a young Danish noblewoman, Kirsten Munk, who bore him eleven children, in spite of which their marriage ended in a divorce in 1630. This made the king extremely bitter and caused endless family disputes. After that he lived together with a commoner, Vibeke Kruse. The sons of the two later liasons received the surname of Gyldenløve ("Golden Lion"), a habit that was to be followed by later kings.

Considering all this adversity it is remarkable how much Christian IV

achieved in the period of peace that lasted until 1643. As the council refused to grant money for a reconstruction of the Kronborg Castle, he did
this on his own account from the much reduced revenue of the Sound
Toll. In 1631 he entered on a plan to double the size of Copenhagen, furnishing it with grand-scale fortifications, which unfortunately he never
saw completed.

In the incorporated area, called New Copenhagen, which included
the Rosenborg Castle, he erected a township of 600 dwellings in one-
storey row houses with individual gardens and wide streets, called Nyboder, for the permanent staff of workers of the royal shipyard, the biggest place of work in Denmark. Here again he was his own contractor,
noting, "If I am not there myself, everything will be a mess."

In 1641 he founded yet another new town, Kristianssand near the
southernmost point of Norway as a convenient haven for naval and merchant ships.

The last of Christian IV's important buildings was the student church
of the Trinity in Copenhagen (next to the state dormitory known as
"Regensen", founded in 1622). The church became an actual trinity,
housing the university library in a room above the church vaults, while
the tower, called the Round Tower, was to hold an astronomic observatory, expressing Christian's holistic conception of religion, humanities
and sciences as various aspects of the entity of God's world. The purpose
of siting the observatory, one of the first state observatories in Europe, in
a tower was to place it above the smoke of the city. The Round Tower,
Christian's last building, has much of the same solidity as the first one,
the Arsenal. It contains a spiral ramp instead of a stairway, but it was not
finished until 1642, when the king was getting old (65), so he never came
to ride to the top of it. Now he had far more serious problems to face.

All this time the Thirty Years' War had continued with undiminished
violence, and Sweden still expanded its territories in Northern Germany,
making the Baltic Sea look like a Swedish lake. The war had lost most of
its original religious aspects and became a mere struggle for power, Catholic France paying Protestant Sweden for its warfare on the Catholic
Hapsburg emperor. In 1642 Denmark offered to mediate in the war, in reality to stop Swedish progress, which brought about a Swedish invasion
of Jutland (in 1643), whose population was again exposed to the horrors
of an enemy occupation. In the next year Christian was himself heavily
wounded in a naval battle, losing the sight of one eye, but it was decisive
for the outcome of this war that the Netherlands had shifted sides because

Christian in 1640 had raised the Sound Toll against the protests of that country. When a Dutch fleet joined the Swedish navy, the entire Danish navy was annihilated, and Denmark was forced to seek peace.

The peace of 1645 reduced Denmark to a second class nation. Sweden took possession of the Baltic islands of Gotland and Oesel as well as of central parts of Norway, making that country narrow along the coast, but of greatest strategic importance was the loss of the Danish province of Halland, stretching from Scania to Norway along the Kattegat, now giving Sweden a wide access to the west and splitting up Denmark and Norway.

The last few years of his life Christian IV spent all his energy on the reconstruction of the navy. Throughout the country oak trees were felled with the effect that drifting sand became an increasing problem.

Christian IV died in the beginning of 1648 leaving behind an impoverished country, his crown pawned to the merchants of Hamburg, and without an agreed succession to the throne, as his oldest son had died a few months earlier.

Christian IV's second son, *Frederik III*, 39, became king only after long negotiations with the state council, which made him sign a very strict coronation charter, not wanting him to behave as autocratically as his father. In theory the council could choose any prince, but in reality this was not possible, as Norway was a hereditary kingdom, not to speak of the trouble it might have caused in Holstein. The council was led by Corfitz Ulfeld, married to Christian IV's favourite daughter, Leonora Christine, a half-sister of Frederik III, and who had for many years played the role of the first lady of the court.

Frederik III who had spent most of his previous life as prince of a miniature state near Bremen, came to Copenhagen surrounded by German advisers, and was met with general suspicion, and his queen, Sofie Amalie from Brunswick, who sought to be a new brilliant centre of the court, was confronted by open hostility. But Frederik was a shrewd politician, which his father had never been. By the issue of underweight coins he took advantage of a quick inflation which enabled him to redeem his father's crown so that he could be properly crowned. Then he began scrutinizing the public accounts of the previous years finding that Ulfeld had made away with large sums for his own good, which caused Ulfeld and Leonora to flee to Sweden. In this way Frederik gradually gained political control of the council.

Even before the flight of this leading nobleman the aristocracy was much weakened. Unusually many of its male members had given their lives in the wars, and out of the remaining 100 aristocratic families, compared to about 500 in the 16th century, a good deal faced economic ruin as their peasants had nothing with which to pay their dues.

The general resistance to illness among people was much reduced, and constantly recurring epidemics killed many. In 1654 about 8000 people died in Copenhagen which was probably more than one fourth of its population. One of the victims was Ole Worm, one of the few doctors who did not leave the city during the plague. He was the first who had taken up the study of the old Runic inscriptions and Icelandic sagas. He had created the first botanical garden as well as the first museum in Denmark, a cabinet of rarities reflecting a strange medley of superstition and empiricism. On one hand he gave an anatomical description of mermaids, on the other he was the first to prove that the unicorn horns originated from the narwhale.

In the first ten years of Frederik III's reign no building activities to speak of took place, but some rich works of wood carvings in the opulent baroque style from exactly this period in such churches as Holmens Kirke (Church of the Navy) in Copenhagen, St. Olai at Elsinore and St. Morten at Næstved, indicate that there was still some wealth in the islands.

The treaty concluding the Thirty Years' War in 1648 confirmed Sweden in her possession of large parts of northern Germany. In 1654 a new, young and very active king, Charles X, ascended the Swedish throne and resumed the endless war with Poland. Frederik III had reconstructed the Danish navy, and created a new fortification, later to be called Fredericia, on a tip of Jutland across from Funen. In 1657 he found the moment opportune to declare war on Sweden to reconquer the land lost in 1645. Charles resolutely left Poland, and marched through Germany and conquered Jutland, including the new fortress. Now once more the fate of Denmark depended on the navy, but the winter of 1658 became extremely cold so that the Danish waters froze up. In the end of January Charles ventured to lead his army of about 12,000 men, half or more on horses, across the ice of the Little and the Great Belts, and in the middle of February he approached Copenhagen. Now both parts wanted a quick decision, Denmark fearing an attack on Copenhagen as Christian IV's new defence line was still not fully completed, and Sweden fearing that a change of weather might isolate its army in the island of Zealand.

Before the end of February a peace was signed at Roskilde: All Danish provinces east of the Sound were to be ceded to Sweden as well as the province of Trondheim, splitting Norway into two parts. As war damage Denmark besides money had to hand over twelve of its largest war ships, completely outfitted. Now Sweden was in possession of one side of the entrance of the Baltic, much to the contentment of the Netherlands and England because of the Danish abuse of the Sound Toll.

However, Charles did not evacuate his army from Zealand, and in August (1658) he broke the peace and made a siege of Copenhagen. For more than two years Denmark consisted only of its capital with 30,000 inhabitants and 6,000 soldiers. The water supplies were cut, but the wells in the city proved sufficient, and salt water was pumped into the moats.

The breach of the internationally agreed peace was immediately met with a reaction from the Netherlands, which feared that Sweden might become the sole power of the Baltic. In October a Dutch fleet fought its way through the Swedish blockade of Copenhagen, bringing in a force of 6,000 professional soldiers as well as provisions.

The winter of 1659 also became so cold that the sea around Copenhagen froze up. After he had received considerable reinforcement from Sweden and Germany, Charles made a decisive assault on the city in the night of Feb. 11, a life and death battle of Denmark. But the defenders had cut channels in the ice, and beat off the attack.

Charles now hoped to starve out the city by occupying the island of Amager, called "the larder of Copenhagen", but the Danish cavalry suddenly charged out of the south gate of the city, and reconquered it. (In 1536 Copenhagen surrendered because it lost Amager). At the same time allied forces from Holland, Poland and Brandenburg began to reconquer Jutland and Funen, while the Norwegian army reconquered Trondheim. Charles hastily left Zealand, only to die a short time later (in 1660). Within a few months the situation had completely changed. An international conference to make a peace was arranged, but to the great disappointment of Denmark none of the big powers intended to let Denmark regain control of both sides of the entrance of the Baltic. France wanted Sweden to resume its war on the Hapsburg emperor, and Holland and England followed the principle "divide and rule". As compensation the province of Trondheim was restored to Norway, and the island of Bornholm in the Baltic, which had been liberated by its own population, was restored to Denmark, but the old Danish provinces of Scania, Blekinge and Halland were lost for good. However, Denmark was reaffirmed in its right to collect the Sound Toll at a reduced tariff. In the war the duke of Gottorp, who owned half of Slesvig and Holstein had sided with his son-in-law, king Charles of Sweden, but a clause in the peace guaranteed the integrity of his lands against Danish confiscation.

Another person who had committed high treason was Corfitz Ulfeld who had acted as a Swedish adviser, but after a charge of treachery by Sweden he fled to Germany, where he died as an outlaw. His wife, Leonora Christine (Christian IV's daughter) was arrested in England in 1663, transferred to Denmark and kept in prison for 22 years without trial. Here she wrote an account of her humiliations, called "A Tale of Woe", which was found 200 years later in Austria, where some of her children had settled. Since its publication in 1869 it has been considered one of the great monuments of Danish literature.

After three years of war Denmark had not only lost one third of its territory, but the remaining part was completely devastated, and the population of this had dropped by at least 15%. In many towns half of the houses were destroyed, and their populations halved. Also many peasants had died from epidemics, and those left had no seeds or livestock. The state of the forests was deplorable, and financially the country was bankrupt.

In September, 1660, political talks were opened in Copenhagen between the king, the aristocracy, the clergy and the citizens. No peasants were invited though they represented 85% of the population. The clergymen and the citizens furiously attacked the tax privileges of the aristocracy and proposed an act to make the country a hereditary kingdom to prevent the aristocratic council from forcing coronation charters on the kings. Now Frederik III exercised pressure by closing the city gates, which meant that the aristocratic leaders were hostages. This made them sign. Of course it was a coup d'etat, but it was only a late political consequence of the fact that the mounted knight had had his day.

On October 18 an official oath of homage to Frederik III as a hereditary monarch was arranged, after which he dissolved the meeting. In their blind hatred of the aristocracy the citizens had forgot to ask for guarantees of political influence, so now the king took the matter into his own hands and made himself an absolute king. He had lost the war, but in the internal political game he had triumphed, having started out from the weakest possible position to emerge with more power than any other king, including Louis XIV of France. In reality, however, the Danish version of absolutism turned out to be a relatively mild one.

Denmark as an
Absolute Monarchy

1660 – 1849

With absolutism came a highly centralized government. The king no longer had to spend time travelling through the country. All important matters were laid before the king in writing, which meant a rapidly growing administration. The court also began to grow with the consequence that Copenhagen doubled its population from about 30,000 in 1660 to more than 60,000 in 1700. Contrary to this the provincial towns stagnated or even declined further. The small country began to grow a "swollen head".

Absolutism also meant that the king was free to take any person into his service, and Frederik did this very provocatively by making his German secretary, Gabel, head of the council – he was both a foreigner and a commoner.

Formerly the council had acted as supreme court too. Now a permanent high court was established with members appointed by the king, and leaving the final decisions to him, at least in theory.

The only class that really benefited from the political change in 1660 was the clergy. Formerly the parsons had not been much better off than the peasants, but now they rose on the social ladder and became an important link in the administration. They had to keep parish registers and announce new laws from the pulpits.

The county governors became civil servants. Land proprietors kept the judicial power over the peasants, but they were also responsible for their taxes to be paid, and if it was not paid, military was placed on the estates to be provided for.

The most urgent question to be settled in 1660 was the financial one. In view of the situation the creditors, whether Danish or foreign, had to accept shares of the crown land at highly inflated prices as payment. In the course of the next decades a considerable proportion of it returned to the state through taxation, because of continued depression and the fact that many of the new land owners were not trained farmers.

Almost half of the Danish territory changed hands in the 1660s which was about the same as after the political change in 1536. A number of the old aristocratic families went bankrupt, whereas others survived as big landowners, mainly by intermarrying and clever administration, but most of them stayed out of politics, boycotting the new rule. Their places in the administration were taken over by commoners or by Germans who became a new group of proprietors, either because they were creditors of the crown, had served as officers in the Danish army, or were members of the Holstein aristocracy who brought with them much demanded capital to reorganize neglected of the devastated estates. They were much feared by the peasants, especially the military ones, who introduced a number of harsh punishments. Few entirely new manor houses were erected. An exception is Nysø in SE. Zealand, built for a citizen of Præstø, in the new baroque style. The former monopoly of the aristocracy to own land with leaseholders had been broken.

Immediately after the peace of 1660 very extensive works were started to reinforce the defence of the country. As a main fortress of Jutland, Fredericia, which obtained its name in 1664, was made into a fortified city with very impressive (and almost completely preserved) ramparts and moats, and in Funen Nyborg was made the main fortification with a new defence line. Copenhagen's defence line was transformed into a zig-zag line of continuous bastions (parts of the moats are to be seen in such parks as the Tivoli and the Botanical Garden). As a special stronghold and headquarters of the army the Citadel was created with a double defence line all around, (which is almost intact to-day).

Perhaps to prove that the king now exercised full control over the finances and to show the outside world that Denmark was far from being bankrupt, great extravagance was spent in this period of poverty on a new throne and new crown regalia, including three life-size lions made of silver coins from the Sound Toll (today in the Rosenborg Castle).

Frederik III also found means for an interesting building between the Castle of Copenhagen and the naval harbour, called "Mars-Lex-Ars". The ground floor was the arsenal of the army (Mars), the second a royal library containing law books, etc. (Lex), and the third a cabinet of rarities and arts (Ars). Frederik III was a great collector and acquired Ole Worm's museum, and his own became the ancestor of all later Danish museums.

(Today the building contains the State Archives).

The greatest Danish scientist of the time, Niels Steensen (latinized Nic. Steno) turned his back on his native country. While studying anatomy in Holland in the 1660s he published pioneer works on the functions of the cardiac muscles and the salivary and tear glands. When he was not appointed professor in Copenhagen he went to Italy, where he published a work about fossils. He thus became the first modern geologist, as he clearly saw that fossils gave information about the origin of the surrounding deposits. A converted and fanatic Catholic he lived an ascetic life with self-torture which probably caused his death in 1686 at the age of 48.

Frederik III died suddenly from pneumonia in the winter of 1670. For the first time in Danish history, the king's oldest son automatically inherited the throne, as *Christian V,* at the age of 24. Inspired from a stay at the court of Louis XIV he transferred his coronation to the chapel of Frederiksborg Castle. Here away from the mobs of Copenhagen, all the splendour of the new crown jewels was exhibited.

Some of his other immediate initiatives were likewise inspired from France. In New Copenhagen right outside the old city he ordered a large square to be laid out, called Kongens Nytorv, i.e. The King's New Square, even today the largest in the city. In the centre of it the first equestrian statue in Denmark was erected depicting Christian V, made by a Frenchman L'Amoureux, while the king's half-brother, Ulrik Fr. Gyldenløve, erected the Charlottenborg mansion (since 1754 the home of the Royal Academy of Art). Nearby a new harbour, the Nyhavn Canal, was dug out. North of Copenhagen the Royal Deer Park was laid out to satisfy his great passion of hunts with beaters and hounds, which he had also learned in France.

Frederik III had had no luck in his attempt to give his son a proper theoretic training, so within a year after Christian V's ascent to the throne, his father's highly intelligent secretary, Peder Schumacher, now 35, who had been the author of the Royal Code, the legal base of absolutism, became the real "lord of the state". He became the leader of the Privy Council and assumed the title of Count of Griffenfeld. Everything went through his hands, and against his verbose arguments Christian V simply gave up.

Griffenfeld became the organizer of the new administration and built up a pyramidal society, topped by the royal family, followed by the illegimate royal sons and their descendants. Next came the members of the

Privy Council (of which Griffenfeld himself was a member) and then the counts and the barons. To be a member of this new nobility the applicant had to possess a certain acreage and pay for the title. For a long time few of the old aristocracy applied for this, while the new land owners lined up wholesale to have their newly designed coats of arms, one more imaginative than the other, licensed.

The old Order of the Elephant was recreated, and a new Order of the Dannebrog (the name of the Danish flag) was instituted. Within this order there were 27 different ranks, all this to make people ambitious to work for the absolute monarch, obtain his grace and climb the social ladder.

With great success Griffenfeld reorganized the deplorable state of the finances, drastically reducing the two dominant items of expenditure, the court and the military. To a great extent the mercenary troops were replaced by a national cavalry. The old aristocracy had never allowed mounted peasants.

These provisions enabled Griffenfeld to reduce the taxation on the land owners and to support industry and trade in Copenhagen. As a result of this the Danish West Indian Company acquired two small islands in the Caribbean, St. Thomas and St. Jan (Virgin Islands).

In one of his great projects, however, Griffenfeld failed. It was his intention to protect and renew the forests, but for this there was no understanding. People continued to fell trees without replanting, and sand drifting increased, mainly in central Jutland but also in N. Zealand.

Griffenfeld was far from being inaccessible to flattery and bribery. Many church ministers had to pay to get a living, so he naturally acquired many enemies. What led to his downfall, however, was his foreign policy.

The ultimate aim of Danish foreign policy was to oust the duke of Gottorp and to regain the provinces east of the Sound. Sweden was allied to France, which in 1672 declared a war on Holland, and in 1674 Sweden attacked Brandenburg (Prussia), but was defeated. In 1675 Christian V decided to enter the war and occupied the lands of the duke of Gottorp. Realizing the strength of France, Griffenfeld still maintained informal negociations with that country, which infuriated the king who ordered him arrested. In his confiscated diary Griffenfeld had noted: "The king answered the French ambassador like a child". Now Griffenfeld was sentenced to death, but pardoned in the last minute, only to live 22 years in prison.

After this nothing prevented Christian V from a direct attack on Sweden (the Scanian War 1675-79). With the aid of the Dutch navy the Danish army invaded Scania and conquered most of it until it was lost again after a terribly bloody battle at Lund in 1676, in which about 5000 Danish and 3000 Swedish soldiers lost their lives. After new conscriptions of men and levies of taxes the war was renewed in Scania the next year, but the king and the army depended on the supply lines from Denmark without which they would be lost. In the end of June the Swedish navy, somewhat stronger than the Danish, approached the Sound, whereas the allied Dutch fleet was detained by contrary wind. In this moment of peril a member of the old aristocracy, Niels Juel, became the saviour of Denmark. Though his instructions said that he was in no way to risk the navy, he took up the fight in the much renowned battle in the Bay of Køge south of Copenhagen. He took advantage of a change of wind he had foreseen. Suddenly he let his ships cross the Swedish line firing their broadsides before the Swedish ships could turn, with the result that the Swedish navy was almost annihilated. But, as usual, the Danish army was not able to make a similar decision. After the peace between France and Holland in 1678 Louis XIV decreed a status quo for Scandinavia after which the Danish forces were evacuated from Scania. The duke of Gottorp was also restored in his lands. The result was as Griffenfeld had anticipated, but he was not released from prison. To seal the peace Christian V's sister was married to Charles XI of Sweden. (In 1683 his brother Jørgen (George) married Anne, later queen of England).

After the war new defence works were undertaken: To protect the growing harbour of Copenhagen the defence line of Christianshavn was greatly prolonged, the castle of Kronborg acquired an outer moat and rampart, and at the easternmost point of Denmark, a couple of bare rocks NE of Bornholm a new fortress, called Christiansø (Ø = island), was created. Earth was brought in by ship, and the only water supply was rain. (To this day it remains a very colourful spot).

To make the heavy taxation more just the first complete land registration was carried out, including an evaluation of the quality of the soil. In 1683 "Christian V's Danish Law" was published to unify and replace the provincial laws from the time of the Valdemars in the 13th century (see page 24). Apart from some very harsh punishments for "crimen majestatis" and witchcraft it was undoubtedly one of the most humane in Europe at the time.

Even the English ambassador Robert Molesworth, who was against absolutism, and in his "Account of Denmark", published in 1694, used

Denmark as an awful warning of this kind of rule, admitted that the Danish laws were more just than the English, and that the safety of the roads was much greater. But in describing Denmark as a backward country he was no doubt right, considering the state of the towns, the roads, etc., and also in pointing out that its intellectual life suffered from lack of freedom.

However, some progress did take place. In the 1660s the first Danish newsletter appeared, and in the following decades the vicar, later bishop, Thomas Kingo (the grandson of an immigrated Scottish weaver) wrote some of the most colourful and vivid poems and hymns ever written in Danish. He dedicated the first volume of hymns to the king in the customary flowery way, but the second volume contained a very personal dedication to the queen, whom he praised because she, though foreign, took the homespun Danish language on her silken tongue, thus indirectly denouncing the king's snobbish attachment to German and French.

In the 1680s both Jews and Calvinists were allowed to settle and hold services in Copenhagen and in the new fortress town of Fredericia, which had been difficult to fill with people in this time of stagnation, and where a number of Catholics had been settled. The Danish bishops were strongly averse to this liberality, but whereas the Catholic congregation was poor, consisting mainly of former soldiers from mercenary troops with their families, there were among the Jews and the Calvinists people with money, skill and initiative, so the economic aspects as always outweighed the religious ones. The first Jews to be admitted were Portuguese, who came by way of Germany. A Jewish cemetery was laid out outside of Copenhagen in 1694, shortly afterwards to be followed by one in Fredericia.

The Calvinists were protected by Christian V's queen Charlotte Amalie, who was a Calvinist from Hessen in Germany and the only queen who did not adopt the official Danish religion. Indulgently she tolerated her husband's mistress at the court. In return he allowed her to erect a church for the growing Calvinist congregation, which mainly consisted of German and Dutch merchant families, but was now supplemented by a number of Huguenot refugees from France, 18 of whom were wigmakers. In the quite monumental church, located across from the Rosenborg Castle inaugurated in 1689, services are still held in German and French.

After Christian IV's township of Christianshavn had been incorporated in Copenhagen the large Church of Our Saviour was built here as an official Lutheran church. It was inaugurated in 1696, and became the finest example in Denmark of the baroque style both as regards architecture and interior (its spiral spire was added in 1750).

Christian V's government greatly profited from the fact that the astronomer Ole Rømer (1644-1710), unlike Steno, returned to Denmark after his stay abroad. In France he had taken a leading part in the construction of the fountains of Versailles, studied the velocity of liquids in tubes and been appointed instructor to the Dauphin, Louis XIV's son. To the question posed by the French Academy why the moons of Jupiter travelled faster when coming closer to the Earth than when moving away, Rømer in 1676 answered that the only possible explanation was that it took time for light to traverse space, which he called the hesitation of light. This revolutionary discovery changed all previous astronomic observations. In 1679-81 he worked with astronomers in London, including Newton, after which he became professor in Copenhagen, where he constructed a number of advanced astronomical instruments. Most of his time he came to spend on what might seem petty jobs, but he was first and foremost a practical man who wanted to be useful to his country. He ended up as police-, fire- and burgomaster (mayor) in Copenhagen as well as judge in the high court. To survey the country he constructed a mileage cart, and furnished the main roads with mile poles of wood, introduced street lights in Copenhagen (which burned whale and seal oil), and he standardized Danish weights and measurements. In 1700 he organized the change from the Julian to the Gregorian calendar, a change that had already taken place in most of Western Europe.

In the 1690s the general state of the country improved a little. The population began to rise, and a number of abandoned farms were resettled. However, the provincial towns remained small and poor, the biggest being Flensborg and Aalborg, each hardly housing 6000 souls. Most of the trade consisted in the export of grain to Norway in exchange of wood and iron. The trade with the colonies Tranquebar in India and St. Thomas in the West Indies, yielded some profit, and industry in and around Copenhagen improved somewhat with paper manufacture as a new element, but in comparison to other countries these items were insignificant. The state budget was brought to balance, but a considerable national debt remained. The only aspect of administration Christian V personally took an active part in was the military which under his constant inspections reached a relatively high standard.

Christian V was a swift traveller. Once, in 1681, he left Copenhagen at 3 o'clock in the morning and arrived at Kolding at 10 in the evening, a distance of about 130 miles together with crossings of the Great and the Little Belt by boat. But his greatest passion was hunting, which caused his death. During a hunt in the Royal Deer Park a stag that had been hunted for a long time by horsemen, beaters and hounds, butted the king, when he was to give it "the coup de grace", and trampled on him. Christian V never recovered from this unroyal treatment, and died within a year, in 1699, at the age of 53.

His son, Frederik IV, born in 1671, ascended the throne at a time of great tension in Europe. England and Holland were closely watching the steps of France in the matter of the Spanish succession. What made the situation of Northern Europe explosive was the fact that all the leading sovereigns were young: King August of the now united Saxony-Poland 30, Frederik IV of Denmark 28, Czar Peter of Russia 27 and Charles XII of Sweden only 17.

The signal to start the Great Northern War (1700-20) was given in 1699 by the 28-year-old duke of Gottorp. To reinforce his part of Slesvig and Holstein he invited the army of his cousin Charles of Sweden to move into his lands which of course brought about a Danish attack. The following year England and Holland sent a united fleet to the Sound which covered the transfer of Charles XII and his main army to Zealand where it landed 20 miles to the north of Copenhagen.

Once more it was seen that the defence of Denmark was in reality impossible because of its geography. The navy busy with the defence of the capital had no chance of transporting the army from the south frontier to Zealand. Again Denmark had to sign a peace treaty, recognizing the status quo, i.e. both the Danish and the Swedish troops had to leave the duke's lands. Much to the annoyance of Charles, England and Holland forced him to retreat from Zealand, but their object to keeping peace in Northern Europe came to nothing, because in the meantime Saxony-Poland and Russia had declared war on Sweden. While Charles conquered most of Saxony-Poland, Czar Peter thrust himself through the Swedish lines to the Baltic Sea and founded St. Petersburg in 1703. By then the long awaited War of the Spanish Succession (1702-14) had broken out. While the flames of war flickered through Europe, Denmark kept a low profile and retained its neutrality until 1709.

In this period the national debt was reduced by ⅔ and Fredrik IV found means to build a summer residence called Frederiksberg on a hill two miles west of Copenhagen, inspired by an earlier visit to Italy, while a considerable part of New Copenhagen was filled with half-timbered

The Castle of Copenhagen, seen from the city around 1700. In the big tower Chr. IV's daughter, Leonora Christine, spent 22 years as a prisoner (p. 64).

The Amalienborg was built c. 1750. (p. 82). In 1794 it became a royal residence (p. 89). The "Marble Church" in the back was not completed until 1894.

The British bombardment of
Copenhagen, Sept. 5, 1807.
The cathedral is on fire (p. 92).
After a drawing by C.V. Eckersberg.

The statue of Hans Christian Andersen in front of the cathedral of
Odense. Andersen was born in
Odense in 1805. During his confirmation in the cathedral in 1819 he
thought more of his new boots than
of the dear God, which later inspired him to write the story of "The
Red Shoes". The cathedral from the
14th century has a fine Gothic interior architecture (p. 28 and 95).

houses for the growing population.

Although Frederik IV had a great taste of love affairs, music and masquerades, he took his work as king very seriously, but he suffered from the lack of a good education, as his father had declared that learning ruined common sense. Unlike his father and grandfather, who always spoke German, he preferred Danish and gave interviews to all, even to peasants, and he took steps to improve the rights of this suppressed class, which made him beloved by the people. But the fact that he wanted to handle every claim from his subjects personally exhausted him physically to such an extent that in 1708 he decided to put the clock of Denmark at a standstill. He left the country with half of the government for recreation in Venice where a magnificent carnival was held in his honour, and from where he returned with an outstanding collection of glass objects (now in the Rosenborg Castle).

But the world outside Denmark had not stood still while he had been away for nine months. Before his departure Russia had promised large compensations if Denmark would join the war with Sweden. In the meantime the Swedish army had been crushed at Poltava in 1709. Now Denmark joined the war without financial subsidies from Russia. A Danish army of 14,000 men invaded Scania, but in this former Danish province a remarkable change had taken place. In the former wars the Danish army had been met as liberators and had been greatly assisted by local partisans and spies. This was no longer the case. Contrary to the stipulations of the peace of 1660 the Danish laws had been replaced by Swedish, and the Danish language had been excluded from the administration, the Church and the schools. In 1710 the Danish army was beaten, and only half of the soldiers regained Zealand.

After this a "peace of death" followed. An "Oriental" bubonic plague, which had worked its way from Constantinople in 1704 up through Europe, reached the Baltic area and paralysed all military activities. It came to Copenhagen in June, 1711. The court, the government and about 5000 well-to-do citizens, including many clergymen and doctors left the city, after which it was completely cut off from the rest of the country for one year. Supplies were left outside the city gates. In July, August and September 22,000 people out of the estimated remaining 65,000 died. But most of the country outside the capital escaped the epidemic.

In 1712 the war was resumed with united attacks on the Swedish possessions in Germany. Once more the duke of Gottorp invited the Swedish army, now in flight, into his lands, which was an open violation of the neutrality guaranteed by the Western powers in 1700. Here the army sur-rendered to the Danes, but soon Charles XII reopened the war with un-expected force after he had suddenly returned from his five-year-long stay in Turkey. As a compensation of the lost provinces across the Baltic he now intended to conquer Norway, but in 1716 a Swedish fleet of 44 trans-port vessels was destroyed by a small Danish fleet, led by the 25 year-old Peder Wessel, then ennobled with the name of Tordenskjold, meaning "Thundershield". The consequence of this tremendous victory was that Norway remained together with Denmark for yet another century. In the same year Czar Peter the Great came to Copenhagen and made his famous ride on horseback up inside the Round Tower.

Charles XII was killed in 1718 outside the Norwegian fortress of Fre-derikssten, perhaps by an assassin. After this the war died down to be concluded in 1720 by the Great Northern Peace, which established a fair balance between Denmark-Norway and Sweden. Sweden had now lost all its provinces beyond the Baltic Sea, except Finland. Russia was now a new important Baltic power. There was no mention of Denmark regaining the Scanian provinces, but it was allowed to incorporate the duke of Got-torp's part of Slesvig, because this was historically part of Denmark, whereas the duke retained his half of Holstein, as this was part of the Ger-man empire. But contrary to what Sweden had done in Scania, i.e. elimi-nating the Danish language, Frederik IV desisted from changing the ad-ministrative language from German to Danish in Slesvig, fearing the re-action from the German land owners and the entire administrative body, with the result that here also the Danish language continued to give way.

In 1721 Frederik IV's queen Louise died, and immediately after her fu-neral he made his mistress, Anna Sofie Reventlow, daughter of a former chancellor, queen. Marrying one of his own subjects was a *faux pas* for a king. This split the royal family up into two antagonistic groups and led to nepotism, as the new queen's relatives and friends obtained high posts.

Generally, however, the financial authorities, now housed in a new government building at 2, Slotsholmsgade (to-day the oldest government building), were efficient. Denmark recovered rather quickly after the war, and the 1720s were a period of great optimism.

In North Zealand Frederik IV erected still another summer residence, called Fredensborg, i.e. "The Peace Palace", overlooking the Lake of Esrum, and undertook a total rebuilding of the Castle of Copenhagen. In reality, however, his greatest building project was the erection of 240 schools throughout the crown land of the country in connection with a reorganization of the cavalry. These schools were built in brick with tiled roofs, markedly different from the peasants farms which were half-timbered with fillings of wattle and daub and with thatched roofs. The schools were for both boys and girls which was remarkable at the time. Although the teachers were poorly educated and badly paid, from now on the level of the education of the peasants rose considerably.

The 1720s also saw the first serious attempt to stop the drifting of sand, as lyme grass and trees were planted along the north coast of Zealand with great success. In Copenhagen a factory began producing Delft ware as there was a great demand of cups and plates 50 years before real porcelain was produced here. At Fredericia a few hundred Huguenot families were settled. After they had been ousted from France in the 1680s, they had lived in Brandenburg (Prussia), but left because they were called up for military service contrary to assurances they had been given. At Fredericia they proved very intensive farmers on their small lots, specializing in vegetable and tobacco growing. In 1736 they inaugurated a church of their own. Like the Jews their influence in the Danish society in the time to come far surpassed their numbers.

In 1721 a missionary, Hans Egede, who had been a vicar in Northern Norway, went to Greenland to preach the Gospel. Much to his surprise he found no Europeans there – they had died out more than two centuries earlier. Undaunted he took up the challenge of converting the Eskimoes, today called Inuits, to Christianity. His children learned the language, and one of his sons translated the Bible into Greenlandic in the 1740s.

In 1722 the first private theatre opened in Copenhagen. It marked the beginning of a real theatrical life, because it was for this stage that Ludvig Holberg, a young university professor, wrote his plays.

Holberg was born in the very international Norwegian city of Bergen in 1684. Having lost his parents at an early age he came to Copenhagen at 17 and passed the usual theological examinations at 19. Living from private tutoring he set out on long wanderings in Europe, first studying in Holland and England and later in Paris and Rome. In France he was overwhelmed by the new critical literature, and in Rome he happened to live with a troupe of actors. In 1717 he became professor in Copenhagen of metaphysics. He hated the subject, but it was the first step on the academic ladder. This tragi-comical situation made him write a long mock-heroic poem, Peder Paars, in which he ridiculed the superstition and the servility of the common people as well as the conceit and arrogance of the upper classes, including the academics. Nothing like this had ever been published in Danish, and it was extremely daring in an absolute monarchy. A trial was prepared, but Frederik IV dropped the case. He was more tolerant than his father and his own son.

After this Holberg was more cautious, but when the theatre opened, he had a "poetic raptus", and in 15 months he produced a comedy monthly. Most of them were written as revues, taking place in contemporary Copenhagen or Zealand, but they have become Danish classics, and are still performed to great applause.

Another professor, the Icelander Arni Magnusson, systematically collected what was left of Icelandic sagas. Many of these parchment manuscripts, then about 500 years old, had been used for shoes, etc., by the poor population of that island. Without his efforts they would have been unknown to us today.

However, the 1720's did not pass without catastrophes. In 1726 most of the town of Viborg, the old political centre of Jutland, was consumed by fire. Before the Reformation in 1536 it had comprised 16 churches, reduced to two Protestant ones, and after the introduction of Absolutism in 1660 it had even lost the ceremonial homage of the new king, but it was still the site of the yearly meetings of the now declining old aristocracy of Jutland. After the fire not one noble mansion was reerected, but its new town hall, inaugurated in 1730 (now a museum) became a model for later ones as preserved in Aalborg (1762) and Randers (1778). The old cathedral was minimally repaired, and was totally rebuilt at about 1870. The other parish church of the town received the altar piece of the Castle of Copenhagen, a great treasure from about 1520.

In October, 1728, a similar conflagration ravaged Copenhagen, where most of the houses were still half-timbered, and at that time of year filled with provisions for the winter. A strong gale spread the fire rapidly and conflicts between the military and the fire brigade hindered efficient counter measures until on the third day the crown prince Christian (VI) took personal command, and prevented the fire from consuming the finest parts of the city close to the King's New Square. Sixty percent of the old city was ruined, equal to forty percent of all houses in Copenhagen, as the fire did not touch the Castle Island, Christianshavn or New Copenhagen. Most of the old churches were destroyed, and so was the town hall and the university with its library and collections, including Tycho Brahe's and Ole Rømer's astronomical instruments, runic stones collected by Ole Worm and a part of Magnusson's Icelandic sagas. This was the greatest loss of cultural heritage that Denmark ever experienced.

To many house-owners the fire meant ruin, but it caused the first (voluntary) insurance company to be founded in Denmark.

Frederik IV, whose six children with Anna Sofie had all died young, interpreted this as well as the great fire of Copenhagen as punishments from God, and came under the influence of a new religious movement, called Pietism, a very personal and sincere kind of Christianity, spreading from Germany. One of his last acts was to issue a law that forbade work on Sundays.

Prematurely aged, Frederik IV died at 59, in 1730, at his small palace of Odense, a former monastery he had transformed. For the first time since the death of Queen Margrethe in 1412, public mourning was genuine. Though little had come out of his reforms to improve the living conditions of the peasants, the people never doubted his intentions. The fact that no new manor houses were erected in his reign indicates that the tax burdens did not affect the peasants alone. An exception was the manor of Clausholm between Aarhus and Randers, his wife Anna Sofie's childhood home, which he rebuilt, and which became her residence after his death.

Christian VI, 31 in 1730, had born a grudge against his father from his childhood because of the bad way his mother, Queen Louise, had been treated. Frederik IV had done everything possible to secure Anna Sofie's position after his death through his will, which Christian VI had signed as a crown prince. But no sooner was he king than he broke it and banished Anna Sofie from the court. An absolute king was absolute only as long as he lived.

Christian VI was a tiny and physically weak person, shy and unapproachable, who had received all his education in German and never learnt Danish. He came much under the influence of his pietist and splendour-loving queen, Sofie Magdalene, from the miniature German state of Kulmbach, and her many attendants. One of them, J.S. Schulin, became postmaster-general with the duty of opening and copying the ex-queen's correspondance. Soon he advanced to be foreign secretary, and as such on one occasion he prevented the king from declaring war on Sweden which meant that Christian VI became the first Danish king for centuries not to lead any wars. Almost everyone in a leading position who had worked for Frederik IV was replaced, which meant a rupture with tradition and a new policy.

Having no veneration for his father's works, Christian VI immediately ordered the barely completed Castle of Copenhagen to be demolished and replaced by the much more magnificent Christiansborg Palace at a time when half of Copenhagen lay in ruins after the fire, and there was a shortage of skilled workers and building materials. The palace was founded on 9,000 beech poles with iron rings, contained more than 600 rooms and was furnished with 18,000 window panes. After ten years of work the king was so impatient to occupy it that in a great hurry it was filled with French carpets, tapestries, chandeliers, etc., while the importation of such luxury goods was otherwise heavily taxed. The project might seem out of proportion, as the entire population of Denmark and Norway hardly exceeded one million, but it was not unique in Europe at that time.

In his short reign of 16 years (1730-46) Christian VI erected more royal buildings than Christian IV had done in his 52-year-long reign. A particularly costly palace built for the queen at Hørsholm in N. Zealand was later demolished, but the funeral palace at Roskilde and the hunting pavillion, "The Ermitage" in the Royal Deer Park, are still to be admired. They were designed by the young architect L. Thurah, who also took part in the shaping of the elegant riding ground of the Christiansborg. So did another young architect, N. Eigtved, who created a mansion for the crown prince (now the National Museum) as there were not enough rooms for him in Christiansborg Palace after he had married in 1743. It was no wonder that the national debt began to grow again in spite of the absence of wars.

In the same period of economic stagnation in Europe the city of Copenhagen was rebuilt after the fire of 1728. This was made possible due to a combination of extreme protectionism and the flow of money from the king, who vastly increased the court with innumerable secretaries, footmen, etc., and whose building activities gave good business to many and attracted so many foreign artisans that they came to constitute more than one third of all artisans in Copenhagen. It had been the government's intention to widen the streets, but as this demanded compensation to house owners, not much came of it. To encourage the rebuilding, half-timbered houses were again allowed, a great number of which still exist together with some finer mansions of better quality.

Economic life was regulated to an extent never attained before or after. Norway was only allowed to buy grain in Denmark, and Denmark only to buy iron goods in Norway. Monopolies for making salt and soap, etc., were given to boiling plants in Copenhagen, and the textile industry expanded so much that the city began to acquire a class of factory workers, whereas the provincial towns remained small and poor. However, a town like Ærøskøbing in the island of Ærø, greatly flourished through organized smuggling across the Baltic as a result of the high Danish tariff barriers. A popular expression for a lie became "a customs-house oath".

In 1732 the Asiatic Company was founded and its main building erected in Christianshavn (now part of the Foreign Ministry). It obtained a monopoly of importing goods such as cotton, silk, spices, tea and porcelain from India and China dutyfree. This soon made Copenhagen an important trade centre for these items, as 80% were re-exported, mainly to the Baltic area, including Russia. In interior decoration a vogue of "chinoiserie" followed.

The Danish trade to the Atlantic was also supported. In 1733 a third island, St. Croix, in the West Indies was bought (from France), and in the following year a Danish trading station was established on the West coast of Africa in Guinea (now Ghana) so that Denmark could imitate the so-called triangular trade of the bigger countries. Ships carried iron goods, guns, liquor, etc., to Africa to be exchanged for slaves, and in the West Indies these were again exchanged for sugar, rum, cotton and tobacco. Importation of such goods from other countries was prohibited. The ships took advantage of the NE-trade wind across the Atlantic and of the Gulf Stream back to Europe. The worst part of the sailing was the passage from Denmark, north of Scotland, to Africa.

In 1736 a national bank was established with the privilege of issuing paper money and of lending money at 4% per annum, and in 1739 the first dry dock for ships was brought into use. Among smaller items now being made in Copenhagen were spectacles, thermometers and barometers. The wearing of wigs was so general that in court records a standard expression for a poor man became that he appeared "in his own hair".

In the 1730s there were very serious cattle diseases in Europe. To prevent peasants from leaving their farms Christian VI put an end to his father's reforms and introduced Bondage, i.e. the peasants were bound to their homesteads, officially to have men for the army, but in reality to secure free labour for the land owners. This meant renewed suppression of the peasants, and enabled many noble proprietors to rebuild their manor houses in a contemporary style, i.e. white-washed or grey facades with big windows, but small panes, and with roofs of glazed blue tiles, while the interiors were richly decorated with tapestries and wall paintings, glass chandeliers, etc. Ledreborg, Lerchenborg and Gavnø in Zealand, Hvidkilde in S. Funen, Dronninglund in N. Jutland and Schackenborg in S. Jutland are good examples. Gardens were laid out in the French style such as the one at Egeskov in S. Funen, and long avenues radiating from the manor houses were planted. The longest was the one leading from Ledreborg to Roskilde, a distance of 4 miles, most of which is still preserved.

Spiritual life was no less regulated than economic. Church attendance and confirmation of children at 14 were made obligatory while all kinds of public entertainment were suppressed. A new generation of pietist vicars fought against the peasants' seasonal festivals, because they usually culminated in orgies of eating and drinking.

Christian VI, himself a devout pietist, had deep religious scruples. After long contemplation he found on one hand moral justification for a possible war with Sweden, on the other he gave up the cruel style of stag hunting his grandfather had learned in France, and sold his hounds even before his hunting pavillion in the Deer Park was completed. But this did not prevent him from introducing the most horrifying kinds of punishments for negligent or obstinate soldiers (daily whipping for several weeks before the execution, etc.) Heavy fines were given for Sabbath-breaking with two exceptions: – military exercise was allowed as well as necessary farm work such as harvesting.

As Pietism called for a *personal* conception of Christianity, it constituted a danger to absolutism. To prevent German zealots to swarm the country it was decreed that all religious meetings had to be led by a clergyman, i.e. a civil servant.

In this grave period a number of musical, scientific and scholarly societies were founded in Copenhagen. Ludvig Holberg, now a professor of history, produced volumes on the history of Denmark, of the Christian Church and of the Jews, but in 1741 he ventured to write a novel "Niels Klim's Subterranean Journey". To avoid the Danish censorship and to reach an international public he had it published in Latin in Germany. Its popularity became so immense that when he had it printed in Danish in the following year, the Pietists refrained from stopping it. Playing on his own name of Holberg, he has the main character drop through a hole of a mountain ("berg") in Norway to a subterranean world where he visits a number of fantastic societies, giving him a chance to praise or to ridicule them. This was the first real novel written in Danish, full of fun and social criticism. As he grew older Holberg took up writing essays on all possible subjects, philosophical as well as practical ones.

Two Danish explorers from this period deserve mention. Vitus Bering joined Czar Peter's new Russian navy in 1703, and in 1725 he was appointed leader of an expedition to find out whether Asia and America were connected. After three years of terrible hardship travelling through Siberia he reached the strait that was to bear his name, and mapped the Asian side of it. But the court of St. Petersburg doubted his observations, and sent him out on a new expedition in 1731. This came to last for ten years, and brought him to Alaska, but resulted in his death from scurvy on Bering Island in 1741.

The other explorer was a young naval officer, F.L. Norden, who was sent out from Denmark in 1737 to Egypt, where he became a pioneer in the exploration of that country, everywhere producing very accurate and artistic drawings. He was the first to map the Nile up to Aswan. 60 years later Napoleon used his maps on his military expedition.

The hard working, but frail Christian VI died in 1746, only 46 years old. His son, *Frederik V,* born in 1723, and especially his queen Louise (a daughter of George II of England) who was often seen in Copenhagen without guards, were met with great relief and enthusiasm, which was increased by a few immediate and spectacular changes: – the guards and the iron chains around the Christiansborg Palace were removed, and the Royal Deer Park was opened to the public. The new king paid little attention to etiquette, and Holberg praised the new regime as blissful.

Few had knowledge of the new king's weak character. His childhood at the stiff court had been devoid of love, but at the age of seven he had the 20-year-old A.G. Moltke as personal tutor. Frederik V as king gave him a large estate in Central Zealand, Bregentved, and made him court-marshall and count. Moltke became the omnipotent leader of Denmark under Frederik V, whose alcoholism was greatly aggravated after the early death of Louise in 1751. A marriage to Princess Juliane Marie of Brunswick in Germany, was quickly arranged, but she never attracted her husband, nor was she ever popular among the people.

However, Frederik V's reign from 1746-66 developed into a relatively happy period of enlightened absolutism with a brilliant flowering of the rococco or Louis XV style in architecture and arts.

Moltke, a hard working and honest man, co-operated well with the government, led by the great statesman J.H.E. Bernstorff, who in the time of the Seven Years' War in Europe and the Colonial War abroad (1757-63) managed the difficult job of keeping Denmark neutral.

Few of Christian VI's laws were changed, but they were now administered in a more liberal way. Frederik V's ascent to the throne coincided with an upward trend in the European economy which made room for costly initiatives, one of the first being the erection of a Royal Theatre in 1747 (the building was replaced by the present one in 1875). Holberg was made a baron, and his funeral in 1754 became a great national event.

To celebrate the 300-year-jubilee of the Oldenburg dynasty in 1748 it was decided to build a dome church in New Copenhagen, but in the hands of the architect Eigtved, it became an entirely new quarter, named Frederik's City, centred around the octagonal Amalienborg "Square". For this place the French sculptor, J. Saly, made the fine equestrian statue of Frederik V, which came to cost more than the surrounding four mansions (royal residence since 1794). These were erected by noble families, one of them by Moltke. Likewise on other conspicuous sites, such as Nos. 26, 34, 42 and 46, Bredgade (= Broad Street) noble mansions were placed, but the great majority of houses were built by citizens, who ranged from timber merchants to blacksmiths. The fronts of the houses had equal heights and levels of windows. Although the church, intended to be built of Norwegian marble, was only completed more than a hundred years later, Frederik's City was not only the largest building project so far in Denmark, but also indubitably the greatest masterpiece of Danish architecture and city planning.

In connection with this project a Royal Danish Academy of Art was installed at the older Charlottenborg Mansion, where it still remains. On unoccupied areas in Frederik's City the first modern operation hospital with 500 beds (125 reserved for poor people) and the first public Botanical Garden in Denmark were established.

A very interesting building designed by Eigtved is Christian's Church at Christianshavn from the 1750s with a theatre-like interior, in reality a true protestant interior with the pulpit mounted over the altar. To raise money for this church the first Danish state lottery was organized. At the same time the older church of Christianshavn, Our Saviour's, was provided with its characteristic spiral spire (300 feet high), designed by Eigtved's rival Thurah, who was busy issuing some of the largest and finest books ever made in Denmark with drawings of Danish buildings and monuments. They were printed by E.H. Berling who founded the newspaper, now called Berlingske Tidende (i.e. Berling's Times) in 1749, which is considered the oldest existing paper in the world today.

Following Norden's travels in Egypt the government sent out a new expedition in 1761 to Egypt, the Holy Land and Arabia, mainly to explore places mentioned in the Bible and to acquire old manuscripts. It was supplemented with a Swedish botanist and a young German land surveyor, Carsten Niebuhr, who was to make maps and astronomical observations. He was the only one to survive the journey, and returned to Denmark i 1767. His copies of the inscriptions in Persepolis furnished material for the later solution of the mystery of the cuneiform writing, and his maps of Yemen, etc., have only been improved in our own time.

In Frederik V's time Danish handicraft, especially within silver-ware and furniture reached a higher level than before. In upper and middle class homes bigger windows gave more light for the appreciation of beautiful objects, which again called for more caution and more refined social conventions. These went hand in hand with the increasing consumption of tea and coffee at the expense of beer. All this reflects the relative prosperity of the time, but powder and perfume were used to eliminate dirt and bad odours, the water in the towns was undrinkable, and the streets filled with rubbish. The great majority of people were poor, but to help the needy a poverty tax on house owners in Copenhagen was introduced in 1762. It was met with violent protests as until then all social work had depended on private charity.

In 1756 a new provincial town, Frederiksværk (værk = works) in N. Zealand was founded. With the water power from the biggest Danish lake Arresø, the manufacture of cannons, cannonballs and gunpowder was sited here (most of which is a museum today, but the town is still the home of Denmark's only steel-rolling mill).

After 42 years of peace the Danish army was in a deplorable state, which became obvious in 1762 when Russia declared war on Denmark. After the death of Czarina Elizabeth, a relative of hers inherited the Russian throne as Czar Peter III. He was of the Gottorp line, and wanted to use the Russian army to regain his ancestors' possessions in Slesvig. Denmark was shaken, but before any battle had been joined, Peter was imprisoned by his wife, Catharina ("the Great"), who agreed to stop the war for a large compensation.

A Hamburg merchant, H.C. Schimmelmann, who organized the large loans of money Denmark needed to raise for the mobilization and the compensation, was soon called to Denmark to be minister of finance. He redressed the financial situation by imposing a head tax, which meant that everybody, whether land-owning nobleman or leaseholding peasant paid equally.

After the danger was over, no reorganization of the army came about, because the landowners had no intention of giving up their right to recruit soldiers, using it as a means of punishment. This meant a conflict with the growing body of officers from a bourgeois background who wanted better motivated men than the most obstinate of the peasants.

After the deaths of the Danish architects Eigtved and Thurah a French architect, N.H. Jardin, was called in. He introduced the neo-classical style, inspired by the excavations of Pompeii. For once a new style came to Denmark without the usual delay. One of the first buildings he designed was the country place of the prime minister Bernstorff, north of Copenhagen in 1760. In the provinces the rococo style lingered on, e.g. in SW. Jutland which experienced great prosperity in the second half of the 18th century for three reasons: – cattle export from the rich marshy lands behind the dykes ("the Dutch corner of Denmark"), the widespread home industry of lace making and the fact that most of the men of such sandy islands as Fanø and Rømø went whalefishing on Dutch ships. When they returned home for the winter they used Dutch tiles as ballast to such an extent that the museum of Tønder today owns the largest collection of those outside of Holland. The rococo style also put its mark on the peasant costumes, especially those of the men (erroneously called "national costumes").

In 1764 Bernstorff called a French (originally Swiss) engineer, Marmillod, to Denmark to construct modern paved roads, called chausées, cut through the countryside in straight lines as far as possible. Over the course of time they greatly improved transport and communication, but they progressed slowly, as they required a great deal of planning and man power. By the end of the century only the main roads of Zealand had been completed. This placed a new burden on the peasants as they were conscripted and not paid for the work.

However, great changes in farming and peasant life were dawning. In the 1750s censorship of writings on economic subjects was abolished. This gave rise to a multitude of magazines and pamphlets calling for reforms. Most of the authors came from the new generation of officers and "rationalist" clergymen. It was the first kind of modern democratic debate in Denmark, and in the 1760s Bernstorff drew the consequences and asked his nephew, A.P. Bernstorff, to carry through a reform on his own estate, which became a pattern for later reforms.

However, Moltke's and Bernstorff's enlightened absolutism came to a sudden end when in 1766 Frederik V died, aged only 42.

Now the absolute monarch was a 17-year-old boy, *Christian VII,* the only surviving son of Frederik V's first marriage, who had an obvious flaw of character. After the death of his mother, when he was three, he had been left in the hands of strict tutors, who found him intelligent. The poor boy learned to act the good pupil, but developed an intense hatred of all the great lords of the court, and became schizophrenic. In the hope of calming the unruly youth and to secure the succession of the dynasty a speedy marriage was arranged in 1766 to one of his English cousins, the 15-year-old Caroline Mathilde, a sister of the later George III. In 1768 they had a son (the later Frederik VI), but a normal marital life was out of question.

In the Christiansborg Palace a court theatre (now theatrical museum) was arranged, where the young king acted with a French troupe, or held masquerades, which culminated in orgies and visits to nearby brothels.

No country in Europe had a more detailed constitution for absolutism than Denmark, but it did not foresee that a king might be mentally ill – or rather its author, Griffenfeld a century before, had not dared to suggest such a case.

Now Denmark was like a ship in a storm without a captain. Moltke as well as most of the administrative and military leaders were sacked, only Bernstorff remained in office due to Russian pressure because talks were going on to buy off the Russian claims on the Gottorp parts of Holstein.

In 1768 Christian VII undertook a journey to France and England. To the great relief of Bernstorff a young German doctor, J.F. Struensee, who seemed to have a very positive influence on the king, was attached to the company. At least the king caused no great scandals on the tour, and loved the ovations he was met with. The English chronicler, Horace Walpole, however, saw through him, and called him a poor figure.

The following year the unhappy queen, Caroline Mathilde, now 18, no doubt suffering from depression, asked Struensee for advice. A modern doctor, inflamed by Rousseau's ideas, he prescribed horse riding instead of medicine. Next he carried out a successful inocculation against smallpox on the sickly crown prince and changed his upbringing radically from luxury to hardship.

From the beginning of 1770 Struensee became the queen's lover, and was installed in the palace with direct approach to the queen's appartment. In the political vacuum the step from being the king's medical adviser to his political adviser was not great. In the spring Bernstorff was dismissed, after which Struensee had the complete political power over Denmark for 16 months, in which he issued some 2000 decrees intended to revolutionize the society.

Although most of these were later revoked, his reign left the Danish administration completely changed. His brother Carl (later to be minister of finance of Prussia) rationalized the financial system, and transferred the revenue of the Sound Toll from the king's privy purse to the state budget, which nobody had ever before dared to suggest. The judicial system was unified for all classes of society. Investigations revealed among other things that a number of old women had spent their entire lives in work-houses where their parents had left them as children.

Most of the other of Struensee's reforms were short-lived. Considering that more than 80% of the population were peasants it enraged most of the land owners that he limited the villeinage of the peasants to 144 days of work a year though A.P. Bernstorff called it "fairly just", and he had no reason to love Struensee because his uncle had been removed from power by him. Equally short-lived was the abolishment of torture in prisons and censorship of the press. The latter led to a flow of pamphlets mocking Struensee, because 20 years before the French Revolution the Danish society was in no way ready for such radical changes. Many of his reforms were badly prepared and their consequences unforeseen as when he introduced free trade, and 2,000 workers in the textile industry of Copenhagen lost their jobs.

When the only park in Copenhagen, The King' Garden, was opened up to the public, it was considered an assault on morality, as it became a place for meetings between young persons, uncontrolled by their parents. And when it was decreed that illegitimate children had to be baptized in the same way as legitimate ones, it was rumoured that it was because the queen had given birth to a girl, whose father was obviously Struensee. On the day of this girl's baptism Struensee assumed the title of count.

One of his reforms became fatal: the abolishment of the royal lifeguard. In reality it had been suggested by the military, but shelved by the former government. The lifeguard was the only part of the army that was commanded in Danish and not in German (whereas the language of the navy had always been Danish). The result was mutiny and demonstrations in Copenhagen, which shook Struensee's authority.

Now the dowager queen Juliane Marie, Christian VII's stepmother (herself a German), took the initiative of organizing a court revolt. The brain behind this was her son's secretary, Ove Guldberg, a former professor of rhetoric. Her son, the heir presumptive prince Frederik, was himself as dull as his half-brother was mad. A rumour was spread saying that

Struensee planned to poison the king.

The coup d'etat was carried out by some adventurous officers in the early morning of Jan. 17, 1772, after a masquerade the evening before. They forced their way into the king's bedroom, where the shocked monarch was intimidated into signing orders of arrest for his queen and Dr. Struensee. In fact these arrests had been carried out at the same time.

Struensee was imprisoned, and a trial against him was opened, but as all charges of unlawful government, corruption, etc. had to be dropped, he was condemned for his intimacy with the queen, which was interpreted as lese-majesty. However, the grounds of the judgment were kept secret. On April 28, 1772, he was publicly beheaded on the Commons of Copenhagen, against protests from England and Russia.

The young queen Caroline Mathilde was confined to the Castle of Kronborg until a British warship fetched her on May 31 after a divorce had been decreed. The four-year-old crown prince had been retained in Copenhagen, but now in tears she had to take leave of the ten-month-old princess. The queen was taken to the Castle of Celle in the province of Hannover, Germany, where she died in 1775, only 23 years old.

The king, whose mental illness aggravated quickly, was brought under constant control of the new regime, led by Juliane Marie and Guldberg, and made to sign everything they wanted, including a number of letters with false dates to legitimate their power. The old statesman Bernstorff would never have consented to this, but to the great relief of the new regime he died in 1772.

Now the political course of Denmark turned 180°. Even the surveying of the farm land, commenced before Struensee's time, was brought to a halt, as it was a necessary preparation for reforms. Guldberg declared that the removal of the yoke of the peasants would make the state tremble. But as the first year of the new regime ended in financial disaster, Schimmelmann had to be called back as a minister of finance, and to repair the relationship with Britain and Russia, A.P. Bernstorff was invited to occupy the chair of the foreign secretary, which his uncle had occupied three years earlier. However, co-operation between this internationally minded progressive man and Guldberg, a conservative Danish nationalist, proved impossible. In 1777 Guldberg took advantage of Bernstorff's pro-British policy in the American War of Independence to dismiss him.

Now Guldberg was as much a dictator as Struensee had been, and he let himself be ennobled with the name of Høegh-Guldberg. His policy was a revival of the state interference and protectionism of Christian VI

(1730-46). Sheltered by this the Royal Copenhagen Porcelain Factory, erected in 1775, developed. A much greater enterprise, however, was the construction of the first canal between the North Sea and the Baltic, connecting the Fjord of Kiel with the Eider River, the fictitious frontier between Slesvig and Holstein. It was the longest canal in Europe at the time (and the forerunner of the Kiel Canal constructed a hundred years later). The construction was only possible, because the whole of Holstein was again a dukedom under the Danish king, as the Russian claims had been bought out (see page 85). Certain sections of the canals are still to be seen.

The "father" of the canal was Schimmelmann, who personnally profited from it as he was a great landowner in that area. But in 1782, two years before the canal was completed, Schimmelmann died, and left Denmark without a firm leader of the finances just at the end of the American War, which shook many commercial companies. State subsidies were paid out to help them with the result that the national debt doubled in 1783.

In 1784 the confirmation of the crown prince *Frederik (VI)*, which should have taken place two years earlier, could not be postponed any longer. This was important because the law stipulated that when confirmed the crown prince was a member of the state council. Juliane Marie had taken all precautions to keep the power, but the 16-year-old prince hated his father's stepmother, and had secretly planned a coup d'etat with Bernstorff, the younger Schimmelmann, and a few other liberal noblemen.

The coup was executed with military precision by the prince alone at the meeting of the council on April 14, 1784. He immediately took the floor, rapidly read a document aloud to the effect that in future all laws had to be countersigned by him, and put it in front of his father, who automatically signed it. After a short physical fight with his uncle he left the confused council with the document in his pocket.

The crown prince appointed a government of liberal landowners, which included a number of the greatest statesmen Denmark ever had. A.P. Bernstorff became the leading figure, and as a foreign secretary he managed to keep neutrality balancing between the great powers even after the outbreak of the British-French wars resulting from the French Revolution. This gave rise to a flourishing trade in the 1790s, when the Danish mercantile marine grew to be the third largest in Europe, second only to those of Britain and France.

The real instigator of the revolt in 1784, however, was another new minister, C.D. Reventlow, who was burning to carry through reforms, which in 1788 concluded in the abolition of the bondage of the peasants, making the Danish peasants free one year before the French Revolution. This opened up for a series of reforms which completely changed not only the ownership of the land and the methods of farming, but also the Danish landscape. Now the land was split up into individual lots, which the peasants were enabled to acquire as owners on easy terms, which meant that in the following decades about half of all farms were moved out of the old villages to be placed in the open land. Much new land which had formerly been placed too far away from the villages, came under cultivation. Gradually the heavy wheelploughs were replaced by smaller, but more efficient ploughs worked by one man and two horses, etc.

The reforms created a middle class of capitalist farmers, but the smallholders, who were just as numerous, obtained little from the reforms, as their lots were too small for a living. To exist they had to work part-time as labourers on the estates, and they continued to be exposed to the landowners' corporal punishments.

In the beginning the great majority of the estate owners of the poorer districts in N. and W. Jutland were strongly opposed to the reforms, but as the demand for grain from Western Europe was still on the increase, the estate owners too experienced prosperity at the end of the 18th century. Although their areas diminished, the remaining parts were now run with greater efficiency, and the instalments from the new farmers meant a safe long-term investment. As soon as this was realized many estates precisely in N. and W. Jutland were taken over by "estate butchers" and split up entirely into new farms.

A fine architectural example of a manor house, one of many built in the late 1700s, is Moesgaard, now the Museum of Aarhus in E. Jutland. Also a number of country places with gardens laid out in the new English, romantic style with artificial ruins, waterfalls, etc., were created, especially by merchants and shipowners north of Copenhagen, but Liselund in the island of Møn, south of Zealand, is the best preserved.

Copenhagen experienced two great catastrophes in the 1790s. In 1794 the main building of the Christiansborg Palace was consumed by fire, after which the royal family acquired the Amalienborg as a residence (see page 82), and the following year one fourth of the city was destroyed in a new conflagration. However, in this time of prosperity the city was almost entirely rebuilt within five years before 1800, and now half-timbered houses were banned, and streets were made wider. The new houses were white-washed or grey according to the prevailing neo-classical style, as can be seen e.g. in Vestergade (West Street) and around St. Nicholas' Church. Two of the finest mansions of this period at Holmens Kanal, designed by the leading architect Harsdorff, are now the headquarters of the two biggest Danish banks.

At the same time the Column of Liberty, commemorating the liberation of the peasants, was erected outside of Copenhagen, where it still remains, but the former country road is now one of the busiest streets in the city, i.e. Vesterbrogade.

The prosperity made the gap between the rich and the poor more conspicuous, and gave rise to a number of social conflicts. Inspired from the French Revolution the first regular strike broke out in Copenhagen in 1794 after the fire of the Palace when there was a shortage of carpenters. They demanded the same pay as the bricklayers, and wanted corporal punishment by their masters to be abolished. The strike was met by military force, but after some years the government gave in.

In 1800 the population of Copenhagen reached 100,000, which was equal to 10% of the Danish population. The total population of the provincial towns amounted to less than 80,000 people, but shortly before his death in 1797 Bernstorff carried through a more liberal trade law, which in connection with the growing export of farm produce broke the stagnation of the towns, which had lasted for 150 years.

After the death of Bernstorff crown prince Frederik, now 29, personally took over the political leadership. This resulted in political reaction and a less flexible foreign policy, although the long-term reforms were continued by Reventlow. To please Russia, some liberal authors were sent into exile, which in reality meant that complete censorship was re-introduced.

To prevent Britain from inspecting and confiscating Danish ships military convoying was started, and in 1800 Denmark, Sweden and Russia formed the League of Armed Neutrality. Britain, wanting to blockade France, sent a fleet led by Parker and Nelson to the Sound, resulting in the Battle of Copenhagen on April 2, 1801. In order not to provoke Britain the Danish navy had not been rigged after the winter inspection, but in a great hurry the ships were anchored up at the entrance of the harbour, unable to manoevre and only furnished with cannons on one side. The fight became very intense, and lasted most of the day until Nelson sent a message to the crown prince that if the Danish fire did not come to an immediate standstill the conquered Danish ships would be burnt regardless of their crews. This ended the battle. Of course it was bluff, but also a blessing as there was little doubt as to the final outcome although the British ships had not yet come within the range of the cannons of the Citadel. The result was that Denmark left the League, which was dissolved anyway because of the murder of Czar Paul of Russia, also in 1801.

The Danish public interpreted the battle as a heroic fight against a superpower, which gave rise to a strong national feeling and a growing interest in Danish history and Nordic mythology, and inaugurated a rich epoch of romantic poetry. For yet some years Denmark was able to carry on a profitable overseas trade with export of grain, mainly to England, but also to France.

In 1803 the transportation of slaves on Danish ships was stopped following a law passed ten years earlier. This measure was soon followed by other countries, but slavery as such in the Danish West Indies was not abolished until 1848.

A very remarkable law was passed in 1805 to protect what was left of the Danish forests which then covered less than 4% of the total area. It was probably the first law of its kind in the world, and it ordered owners to replant as much land with trees as were felled. Gradually the woodland began to increase (today 11% of Denmark is wooded).

In 1807 the situation of Denmark became hopeless as the Danish naval and merchant marine became the bone of contention in the European war. After Napoleon had conquered Germany and concluded the Tilsit agreement with Russia, Britain doubted if Denmark would be able to resist Napoleon, and was firmly determined not to let France get hold of the Danish ships.

In Denmark opinion was strongly pro-British in spite of the episode of 1801, and the entire Danish army of 30,000 men was lined up along the south frontier to meet a possible French attack. Even if Jutland had been conquered as in former wars, it was from a Danish point of view quite inconceivable that Napoleon should ever get hold of the Danish navy which would in any case be preserved to guard the Danish islands. From London, however, things looked different.

In August, 1807, the British arrived with a large fleet in Danish waters demanding that the entire Danish navy should be handed over to the British against compensation after the war. As this ultimatum was refused, a professional British force of 31,000 men under the command of general Wellesley, later Duke of Wellington, was set ashore north of

Copenhagen, as an attack from the seaside had proved so difficult in 1801. As in similar earlier cases, e.g. in 1701, the Danish army had no chance of relieving the capital, but the situation was far from being regarded as hopeless, because Copenhagen was strongly fortified. But this time a new weapon was brought into use, i.e. the Congreve fire-rockets, which had been developed, but not yet employed. It meant that Copenhagen was the first city in world history to be exposed to a rocket bombardment. It started in the evening of Sept. 2, and continued for three nights. Many of the inhabitants fled to the island of Amager. In the morning of Sept. 5 the cathedral caught fire, and this started a conflagration which also consumed the university and the surrounding densely populated area, covering 10% of the city. Few houses in the city were untouched. On Sept. 7 Copenhagen capitulated, and on Oct. 21 the British sailed away with the Danish navy consisting of 69 ships after the shipyards had been destroyed. On Oct. 31 Denmark signed an alliance with France, and on Nov. 4 Britain declared war on Denmark officially. After this the Danish colonies were occupied, and all the merchant ships were confiscated.

British ships now controlled the Danish waters making journeys between the Danish provinces dangerous, but the worst consequence was serious starvation in Norway which was cut off from its usual supplies of grain. The Danish contribution to the warfare consisted mainly in attacks by small gun-boats on the convoys carrying grain and timber to England and weapons to Russia. But the British operations around Denmark were exposed to other dangers. On Christmas night of 1811 two British warships were washed up on the sandbars off the west coast of Jutland at Thorsminde, where 1600 men were drowned.

In 1808 the mentally ill, but still nominal King Christian VII died, from which time his son, Frederik VI, de facto king since 1784, became king in name as well.

What caused the death of Christian VII was the shock he received when he saw Spanish troops entering Denmark. In reality they were called in to reinforce Denmark against the British. When Spain soon after revolted against the French, the Spanish troops were picked up by British warships and sailed home to assist in the anti-Napoleonic fight there.

After 1807 Denmark became so impoverished that the state declared itself bankrupt in 1813. The banknotes were exchanged for new ones, reduced to 1/6 of the former value, and in the following year Denmark had to ask for a separate peace as a united Swedish-Russian-German army invaded Holstein after Napoleon's retreat from Moscow and his defeat at

Leipzig.

Denmark was forced to hand over Norway to Sweden in compensation of Finland which Sweden had had to yield to Russia. Norway was no longer a poor province. Its population had greatly increased in the 18th century, and developed a national identity so that Sweden had to accept a Norwegian democratic constitution to deal with its interior affairs. To the Danish people the loss of Norway after a union that had lasted for 450 years was a hard psychological blow. However, the Faroe Islands, Iceland and Greenland remained with Denmark. The small island of Heligoland in the North Sea was yielded to Britain, but the Danish colonies were so insignificant to Britain that they were restored to Denmark, but no compensation was paid for the Danish ships nor for the damage inflicted.

One by one all the formerly rich commercial companies in Copenhagen went bankrupt, especially during the international crisis of 1819-20 with great unemployment as a consequence. Though measures were taken to distribute food and fuel to the poorest, the social distress was apalling. Farms were sold for nothing, and the state had to take over a number of estates. In 1822 the prices of farm products reached the lowest level since about 1740. After that economic life slowly improved.

In such a time it is no wonder that political reaction aggravated all over Europe. In 1821 a lecturer who demanded democracy, if necessary through a revolt, was imprisoned for life, only to be released in 1848. It is a greater wonder that the administrative reforms went on as if nothing had happened. In 1814, the most sinister year, a School Act was passed. It had been prepared for 25 years so that throughout the country school houses were ready, and teachers' training schools had been founded. The law demanded compulsory education of all children between 7 and 14 years of age, but allowed private schools and private tutoring. It brought Denmark into a leading position of popular education in Europe. It remained in force, unchanged, until 1935.

Another law, passed in the same year, gave Jewish citizens full civilian rights, e.g. to own property, though with one exception: – they could not become civil servants (until 1848). The unique element about this was that it was not recalled during the period of the political reaction and growing nationalism in Europe after the Napoleonic Wars.

The reconstruction of Copenhagen turned out to be a very slow process. A new town hall was inaugurated in 1815 (now the city court), but the reconstruction of the cathedral and the Christiansborg Palace (destroyed in 1807 and 1794 respectively) lasted until 1828. All of these three buildings were erected in a very serene classical style by the architect C.F. Hansen. The fourth monumental building, the university, inaugurated in 1836, was called "gothic" under the influence of the neo-gothic West-minster Palace in London, but real Victorianism did not appear until about 1860.

In 1819 a paddle steamer was bought in Britain, and began a regular route between Copenhagen and Kiel (in Holstein) carrying passengers, mail and freight. But apart from this little of modern industrial develop-ment reached Denmark until the middle of the century.

Copenhagen remained a fortified city which meant that the growing population had to be housed inside the ramparts. Most of the citizens' new houses had plain facades, but interiors were often provided with wall paper, a novelty at this time. But these front houses hid the fact that the many poor people were crowded in back buildings, to which extra storeys, attics, etc., were added in half-timbering, making the court-yards still darker. The water supply came unpurified from nearby lakes, and the lack of sewers made the streets dirty and stinking, attracting hordes of rats.

However, this poor capital was the focal point of the most remarkable epoch of Danish cultural life, called the "Golden Age". In 1820 the scien-tist H.C. Ørsted proved the existence of electro-magnetism, which laid the basis of all later means of communications such as the telegraph and the telephone.

The philologist Rasmus Rask became a pioneer in the study of lan-guages. In 1811 he published a book on Icelandic and Old Norse and in 1817 one on Anglo-Saxon after he and Grundtvig (see below) had studied the Beowulf poem before it was translated into any modern language. Later he wrote works on a wide range of both dead and living languages such as Finnish, Hungarian, Zend and Sanskrit, Singhalese, etc.

Within the field of non-classical archaeology, too, a Dane became a pioneer. In 1819 the state Museum of Nordic Antiquities was opened, and its leader became C.J. Thomsen, a Copenhagen merchant, who in-vented the terms "stone, bronze and iron ages" in 1836, choosing the names according to the hardest materials used by man for tools and weapons.

To Danish people, however, the Golden Age mainly refers to arts and letters, first of all paintings. A generation of talented painters born at the beginning of the century were tutored by the enthusiastic leader of the Royal Academy of Art, C.V. Eckersberg. Nowadays Christen Købke is considered the most outstanding of these, perhaps because in some of his works from the 1840s he seemed to foreshadow impressionism, but it was another, J. Ths. Lundbye, who created the romantic picture of the Danish landscape, kept in the hearts of all Danes even today.

The only internationally known Danish artist at the time was the sculptor B. Thorvaldsen, who lived most of his life in Rome. His first work of fame became a model for the Lion of Lucerne (in 1819) commemorating the Swiss guards fallen in Paris in 1792. After this he executed a number of statues, e.g. of Copernicus and Poniatowski in Warsaw, Gutenberg in Mainz, Schiller in Stuttgart and Byron in Cambridge, but his most extensive work was his statues of Christ and the apostles in the recreated cathedral of Copenhagen.

At the Royal Theatre August Bournonville created the national Danish ballet. Whereas Thorvaldsen's father was from Iceland, Bournonville's father was an immigrant Frenchman.

In the 1830s Hans Christian Andersen began writing his fairy tales and Søren Kierkegaard his extensive philosophical works. Andersen, whose father was a poor shoemaker, in his magic world always sided with the weaker, i.e. the child, the innocent and the disregarded, and thus indirectly spread an understanding of the poor and the minorities. Kierkegaard, whose father was a rich wool merchant, became the great individualist among philosophers. He stressed the individual responsibility in any act you do or omit to do, and ended up with a series of attacks on the established Church, advocating the view that religion is a personal matter, and that there should be no institution between God and the individual.

However, the author who came to influence Danish way of living and thinking more than any other was N.F.S. Grundtvig (1783-1872), son of a vicar and himself a vicar, who produced innumerable songs, hymns, essays and historical works. In contrast to Kierkegaard's individualism he stressed the fact that nobody is an island. You belong to a people, and you are part of a national heritage (the Danish heritage). His idea was that Denmark should reach a stage where "few have too much, but fewer too little". He vigorously attacked the old grammar schools where so much had to be learned by heart, and suggested voluntary schools for young people who should live in groups with their teachers for some months, learning about the world by way of "the living word". This led to the erection of a great number of "folk high schools" from 1840 and onwards, the importance of which can hardly be overestimated.

After the short-lived French revolution of 1830 Frederik VI much to his annoyance found himself obliged to institute advisory provincial councils, elected by property owners, in the 1830s. If nothing else they became a kind of training school for future democratic politicians. Another progressive step was the prohibition of the use of torture in the prisons in 1837.

In 1839 Frederik VI died after having ruled for 55 years. Because he had no sons, he was succeeded by his cousin, *Christian VIII*, a handsome and intelligent man, now 53. The improving economic conditions and common literacy as a result of the school act of 1814 resulted in a growing demand for democracy, and in 1841 an important law introduced local self-government, but a growing national conflict in Slesvig and Holstein came to block further steps.

Heralding a new time to come, the Tivoli Amusement Gardens were established right outside the city gate of Copenhagen in 1843, the Burmeister Shipyard began to build steamships, British engineers constructed a railway from Copenhagen to Roskilde, and the Carlsberg Brewery was founded in 1847.

In 1838 the aged sculptor, Thorvaldsen, had returned home after his lifelong stay in Rome. A museum was erected next to the Christiansborg Palace to hold his models as well as his collection of classical antiquities. The building itself, gaily painted yellow in the midst of the grey, conservative city, expresses the optimistic spirit of the 1840s. It was decorated with a monumental frieze, depicting Thorvaldsen's arrival in the habour of Copenhagen, but he is not met by the king and the leading figures of the society, but by his friends, i.e. other artists and writers (including young Andersen) as well as by the common people so that also seamen and workers are shown in full size portraits. Another outstanding feat is a boat with only women in it (i.e. the leading actresses of the Royal Theatre). All this makes it an outstanding piece of European art from before the revolutions of 1848. (The frieze was renewed in the 1950s).

Denmark had again become a seafaring nation. Hundreds of sailing ships from small towns as Dragør, Ærøskøbing and Aabenraa reached the farthest destinations of the world, but Copenhagen never reached the position as a centre of colonial trade it had held before the Napoleonic Wars. The turnover of the port in the 1790s was only reached at about 1880. As a consequence of this the small Danish colonies in India and Africa were sold to Britain in 1844 and 1850 respectively.

In the beginning of the crucial year of 1848, Christian VIII died, leav-

A bourgeois family in Copenhagen, 1828. Painting by Emil Bærentsen.

A street in the town of Faaborg, S. Funen, with half-timbered (or "framed") houses, mainly from the 18th century.

Painting by A.H. Hunæus, 1862, in the Copenhagen City Museum, showing people promenading on the rampart on a certain spring evening.

The final Danish retreat from the 1000-year-old defence line of Danevirke on Feb. 5, 1864 (p. 100).

ing the throne for his son of his first and very unfortunate marriage, *Frederik VII*, 40, who was generally distrusted because of his peculiar mind. On one hand he was a jolly drinker with two divorces behind him, and now lived with a commoner (whom he married "to his left hand" in 1850, and gave the title of countess), on the other a keen amateur archaeologist. As such he had been the first to point out that there had been cannibalism in Denmark in the Early Stone Age, which few in Europe at the time were ready to accept.

Before Frederik VII was crowned, a public demonstration in Copenhagen on March 21, 1848, demanded democratic rule. This peaceful march, led by the magistrate of the city, overthrew the absolute rule which had lasted since 1660, because in contrast to other European capitals it was not met with military power. The new king appeared on the balcony of the Christiansborg Palace, and promised a democratic constitution.

But at the same time representatives from the dukedom of Slesvig-Holstein demanded not only a free constitution, but also that Slesvig was incorporated into the German Federation. Nobody in Denmark wanted sovereignty of Holstein, but to give up the originally Danish province of Slesvig was out of question. Although the language of the administration, the church, the courts, and the upper class had been German for centuries, the rural population had retained its Danish tongue until schools became common. But with the schools (in the German language) the ability to speak only Danish became synonymous with being uneducated. Thus in the first half of the 19th century a complete change of language from Danish to German had taken place in the southern half of the province, i.e. south of Flensborg, whereas the northern half was still Danish speaking.

The controversy in 1848 led to a military confrontation in which also Prussia became involved, and which came to last for three years though with intervals of armistices, called The First Slesvig War, 1848-50. After a series of defeats the Danish army was secretly concentrated in the fortified city of Fredericia, from where it made a victorious sortie on July 6, 1849. More important, however, was the fact that a conservative reaction had set in all over Europe after the revolts of 1848, after which few governments wanted to support insurgents or to change the frontiers of 1815. This made Prussia withdraw from the war, and in 1850 an international conference in London confirmed the integrity of the Danish monarchy, i.e. a status quo that solved nothing.

After the war a monument was erected at Fredericia, idealizing the common soldier. Formerly all such monuments in Europe had shown the military leaders. This was a new democratic manifestation.

Denmark
under a Democratic
Constitution

after 1849

During the First Slesvig War a Danish constitution was drawn out, and a parliament consisting of two chambers was elected by all men over 30 with a household of their own. Although there were some restrictions as to age and income to be a member of the upper house, the constitution was extremely liberal for its time. The king retained the right to appoint ministers, but laws were to be passed by a majority in the two chambers. The legislative, executive and judicial powers were separated, civil and religious freedom was secured, and censorship of the press was forbidden. The administration of justice was made oral and public.

This liberal constitution was signed on June 5, 1849, by a very reluctant king Frederik VII, who feared its consequences internally and especially externally with good reason.

The new liberal rule, however, opened up for a modern development of the country. Copenhagen was no longer to be a fortified city, and was allowed to expand beyond its ramparts, but not before a cholera epidemic in 1853 killed 4% of its population of about 150,000. This led to the erection of a large municipal hospital with modern plumbing for gas and water outside of the ramparts. Postage stamps, state telegraph and gas lights in the streets were introduced. In 1857 a liberal trade law abolished the artisans' guilds and made way for industrial production. The first private bank was founded, and the Sound Toll was abolished, mainly as a result of American pressure. Soon the biggest provincial towns of Odense, Aalborg and Aarhus passed the mark of 10,000 inhabitants each.

The great political issue was the future constitution of Slesvig-Holstein. In 1863 the Danish Parliament decided to cut the Gordian knot by extending the Danish constitution to include Slesvig, which meant a separation of Slesvig and Holstein. Two days later king Frederik VII died before he had signed the law.

Frederik VII was the last of the Oldenburg dynasty, which had ruled Denmark since 1448, but the line of succession had been planned and accepted by the great European powers to the effect that prince Christian of Glücksburg, who descended from Christian III and had married a cousin of Frederik VII, became king under the name of Christian IX.

Now its was up to the new king to sign the law, and although he feared that it might lead to a war with Prussia, the public pressure was so strong that he finally signed it. Nobody had suspected the resoluteness of Bismarck, the new political leader of Prussia. On January 16, 1864, he wired an ultimatum to Denmark that if the law was not repealed within 48 hours it meant war not only with Prussia, but also with the Austrian empire. This was of course practically impossible, but the Danish government declared that it would resign if the law was not withdrawn. However, the German military machine was already on the go.

For the last time the Danish army (of 40,000 men) took up positions along the 1000 year-old defence line of Danevirke against a united German force (of 57,000) armed with modern breech-loaders. When the marshes to the west and the fjord of Slesvig to the east froze up, the Danish army secretly retreated in the night of Febr. 5. In spite of terrible hardship in the cold night the retreat was carried through to perfection. The best military planning of the Danish army was always retreats. A new position was taken up at Dybbøl across from the island of Als, northeast of Flensborg, where the trenches were overrun in a bloody battle on April 18. After the loss of the island of Als on June 29 an armistice was arranged.

The situation was typical of Danish wars. The main province of Jutland was occupied by the enemy, this time the Germans, but they were not able to proceed further as the Danish navy commanded the waters after it had beaten an approaching Austrian squadron sent from Trieste.

In the peace talks Denmark got little international support. Queen Victoria and the British government were anti-French and pro-German, and the Russian czar looked upon Denmark as the one who had broken the old order and even tried to extend democratic rule (i.e. to the province of Slesvig). On the other hand Russia wanted in no way to let Germany get direct control of the entrances of the Baltic Sea. On Oct. 30 Denmark signed the Peace of Vienna demanding Denmark to hand over Slesvig-

Holstein to Germany. The new frontier was drawn just south of Ribe and Kolding, leaving a Danish population of about 175,000 under foreign rule. Only two years later Prussia and Austria had to fight a war over the booty, after which Slesvig-Holstein was entirely incorporated in Prussia. From 1865 to 1905 more than 55,000 Danes from this region emigrated to the U.S.A. Danish schools were forbidden, Danish editors persecuted, and state money from Prussia was granted to buy up Danish farms. But the harder the suppression, the stronger the opposition to it. Only the town of Flensborg changed its character from a Danish to a German town after it became a strong military and naval base.

The Second Slesvig War of 1864 reduced Denmark to its smallest area ever, i.e. 39,000 sq km.s (= 15,000 sq miles) with a population of 1.7 mill. people. The liberal leaders were held responsible of the disaster, and in 1866 the parliament, still paralyzed by the shock, passed an amendment to the constitution according to which half of the members of the upper house were to be elected by owners of large properties. From then on Christian IX took his ministers from the comfortable conservative majority of this house, which led to a 30-year-long struggle with the lower house, dominated by "the Left", organized as a political group in 1870 by the farmers.

The economic life of Denmark was not paralyzed for long. The motto became:- "What was lost outwardly has to be won back inwardly". A grand-scale reclaiming of land was soon started by E. Dalgas, a military engineer of French Huguenot descent. More than 20% of Jutland was practically uninhabited. Now the breaking up of this heath land was commenced as well as the draining and damming up of marshy areas. Thousands of new homes were established in central and western Jutland with the assistance of the "Heath Society", which explains that the Danish contingent of emigrants to the U.S.A. was relatively small (except for the emigration from the Slesvig region mentioned above). In the great period of European emigration across the Atlantic 1868-1914 "only" every tenth Dane left whereas for example every sixth Norwegian did so. But the life of those who went west in Denmark, planting firs and spruces and living from the income of a few domestic animals, was in no way easier than of those who went west in America.

For the big estate owners the 1870s became a glorious period. Not only were they now back in political power, but they also profited from a growing demand for grain in Europe. A number of manor houses in the Victorian style were built, such as Frijsenborg north of Aarhus. They were operated by hundreds of poorly paid farm labourers and servants. However, towards 1880 an international agricultural crisis set in due to ever increasing imports of grain on steamships from the plains of America and the Ukraine. The big estates compensated by exporting butter, but ruin threatened the smaller farmers all over Europe. In 1882 the first co-operative dairy in the world was founded in SW. Jutland. To have sufficient fresh milk for a daily production the farmers united to have their milk collected daily. The co-operative idea had originated at Rochdale in England, but now it was applied to production instead of distribution. The idea spread like wild fire, and was followed up by co-operative bacon-factories, egg-collecting companies, etc. This was an indirect effect of Grundtvig's Folk High School movement (see page 95), because it had given the Danish farmers a wider horizon and taught them to co-operate. One important new crop was the sugar beet. Around 1900 Denmark had reached a leading position in the world as a manufacturer of first class animal farms products.

Although Denmark was still primarily an agricultural country a complete transformation from a natural to an industrial economy took place in the last third of the 19th century. Soon railways reached even the most remote parts of the country. The main lines were constructed by the state, and the local connections by private companies. On the west coast of Jutland the port of Esbjerg was founded to facilitate trade with Britain. Factories grew up in all the towns, and under the leadership of C.F. Tietgen, manager of the leading bank, companies were merged into big corporations, such as the United Steamship Co. and the United Sugar Factories. In 1881 the Bell Telephone Co. opened a central in Copenhagen, but after only one year Tietgen bought it, after which telephone service became a private company under special state supervision – a typical Danish construction.

From 1850 to 1900 Copenhagen's population grew from about 150,000 to almost 500,000. Most of the newcomers were industrial workers who were lodged in new, but very small flats without sanitary installations. The rent was high, amounting to 1/3 of a worker's income. But many were unemployed in the winter, and poor relief meant loss of civil rights. The later labour leader, Th. Stauning, related how his father lost his right to vote. In spite of seasonal unemployment he had never applied for public assistance, but one night his wife became so ill that he asked for a visit of the doctor for the poor, for which he was unable to pay. One of the greatest dangers was tuberculosis, especially for those who suffered from malnutrition.

After the Paris "Commune" socialist agitators became active in Denmark. In 1872 a public socialist meeting was attacked by mounted police, and the leaders were sent to prison, where in the course of a few years they lost their general health and eventually their teeth. Gradually, however, trade unions were formed, and their leaders were less revolutionary than the first agitators. In 1884 two "Social Democrats" were elected to the lower house.

One positive fact in the rapid development of Copenhagen was that, in contrast to most other big cities of Europe (e.g. Vienna, Paris and Antwerp) the former ramparts were made into public parks, including a new Botanical Garden. In 1875 a new Royal Theatre was built. In 1884 a fire reduced the main building of the Christiansborg Palace, home of the government as well as the parliament, to a ruin. For the next 20 years it remained a ruin since the majority of the lower house looked upon it as a symbol of the suppression of the people, and refused money for its reconstruction. But the danger that all the state collections of cultural value had been exposed to (as they were all concentrated in and around the palace), led to the erection of a number of new museum buildings, such as the Royal Museum of Fine Arts, as well as new library and archive buildings.

In this connection a special mention must be given to the owners of the Carlsberg Breweries I.C. Jacobsen and his son Carl Jacobsen. The former had paid for the reconstruction of the Frederiksborg Castle in N. Zealand, which had been greatly damaged by a fire in 1859, and made it into a museum, containing the largest portrait gallery of Denmark. He had also created a large foundation to support Danish science. Carl Jacobsen wanted to make Copenhagen "the Florence of the North". He donated large sums for monuments and other works of art, and erected his own museum, The Carlsberg Glyptotek, which houses an outstanding collection of classical antiquities as well as of French impressionism.

The paralysis of the intellectual life after 1864 came to an end in the 1870s when a literary critic, Georg Brandes, a declared atheist of Jewish descent, became the spiritual father of Danish Radicalism. He inspired a new class of authors mainly from the provinces to write in a more "realistic" style. A number of their works were translated into other languages such as German and French, but to penetrate the English speaking part of the world has always been difficult for writers from small language areas. A number of female writers also appeared, and in 1882 women were allowed to study at the university.

Politically Denmark was firmly ruled by the leader of "the Right", J. Estrup, an intelligent and efficient estate owner, from 1875 to 1894. To obtain money for a new defence line around Copenhagen he had to issue a number of budgets as provisional laws, which were never passed by the lower house. But in the 1890s things began to change. Fearing the progress of the Social Democrats a meagre old age provision was introduced, and trade unions carried out successful strikes. In response the employers formed their own organization. In 1899 the situation exploded in a general lock-out which lasted for four months and ruined many workers financially. The result was an agreement, called "the constitution of the labour market", which gave the employers the right to employ and dismiss employees, but accepted the unions as partners of negotiations and allowed duly noticed strikes and lock-outs.

In 1901 the old King Christian IX took the consequence of the changing times by appointing a government from the majority of the lower house. Since then Parliamentarism has been the rule which means that a government that is met by a vote of no-confidence in the lower house has to resign.

Christian IX was called the grandfather of Europe. His son Vilhelm (alias George I) sat on the throne of Greece, while his oldest daughter, Alexandra, was married to Edward VII of Britain. His second daughter, Dagmar (alias Maria Feodorovna), was married to czar Alexander III of Russia, and in 1905 he even saw a grandson, Carl, chosen as king Haakon VII of Norway, when this country finally reemerged as an independent nation. When Christian IX died in 1906 at the age of 88, he was succeeded by his much more liberal son, Frederik VIII, who survived his father by only six years. His son, Christian X, was king from 1912 to 1947.

In the field of science and technology things began to happen fast around the turn of the century. In farming industry reapers and self-binders were spreading, the dairies adopted the centrifuge, and from about 1890 the bicycle became common and much beloved in Denmark. It became a symbol for a new freedom of the youth which also took up a number of sports of which football (soccer) became particularly popular. The first automobiles appearing in the 1890s remained but a thing for the few. Most important of all was electrification, which spread rapidly after 1900. In 1903 a Dane, Dr. Niels Finsen, received the Nobel Prize for his treatment of skin diseases by light, and in wireless telegraphy Danes, too, were pioneers. In 1906 the first regular flight in Europe took place in

A Danish co-operative dairy at about 1900 (p. 102).

29 Danish naval ships were scuttled on Aug. 29, 1943, a few minutes before the Nazis arrived to get possession of them (p. 109). The crane is from 1747.

The Town Hall of the city of Aarhus, built 1938-42, was met with great opposition as it contrasted to traditional Danish brick buildings as those nearby, only ten years older (p. 107).

The Liberty Column, commemorating the liberation of the peasants in 1788, was erected in 1797 outside the west gate of Copenhagen. Now it remains surrounded by modern buildings such as the SAS-hotel Royal from the 1960s. (p. 90).

Denmark, and in 1912 the first Diesel engine ship in the world was launched in Copenhagen.

After the political change in 1901 money was granted for the reconstruction of the Christiansborg Palace just as the new Copenhagen Town Hall had been completed. More outstanding as an architectural and technical achievements was, however, the Central Station of Copenhagen, completed in 1911. New laws introduced secret voting, income tax, unemployment insurance and the metric system, which had, however, been applied to money since 1875. But a complete revision of the constitution was not carried through until 1915, when everybody above 25, including women, obtained the right to vote.

In the meantime World War I (1914-18) had broken out. Denmark immediately declared itself neutral, but after German pressure Denmark mined the entrances to the Baltic, which was tacitly accepted by Britain. In 1916 the German High Sea Fleet ventured a confrontation with the British Grand Fleet in the Skagerrak northwest of Jutland, called the Battle of Jutland (May 31-June 1). The British suffered the heavier losses, but the battle put an end to German dreams of maritime domination. In desperation Germany declared unrestricted submarine warfare from 1917. To Denmark this meant a serious shortage of coal and raw materials, unemployment and social distress, whereas some people made quick profits from exporting canned food of poor quality to Germany. Hundreds of Danish ships were sunk, and many seamen lost their lives. Worst of all, however, was that 6000 Danish men from North Slesvig lost their lives as German soldiers, forced to fight for a cause which was not theirs. This loss was proportionately far higher than for any other region of Germany!

During World War I Denmark was practically cut off from its overseas territories. This resulted in the sale of the three small Danish West Indian Islands (called the Virgin Islands) to the U.S.A. in 1917, and in 1918 Denmark accepted Iceland as an independent nation (though with the Danish king as its sovereign until 1944). But these losses were overshadowed by the fact that the Versailles Treaty of 1919 maintained the right of the people of Slesvig to decide its own nationality by a plebiscite. The result was that Northern Slesvig was reunited with Denmark in 1920 with a 75% majority. A territory of 1500 sq.miles with a population of 165,000 was thus added to Denmark.

The incorporation of North Slesvig (from now on called South Jutland) meant a heavy economic burden, as it was the least developed corner of Germany, but grants to solve these problems were carried through by a unanimous parliament. But readjustment of the economic life after the war unleashed violent demonstrations and labour conflicts, resulting in a eight-hour-workday in 1919. In 1921 the largest Danish bank collapsed.

In the 1920s the governments alternated between the Liberals, supported by the Conservatives, advocating economic liberalism, and the Social Democrats, supported by the Radicals, advocating state intervention for social reasons. When the first Social Democratic government was formed in 1924, it included a woman, which was unprecedented in the western world. The government was headed by an unskilled tobacco worker, Th. Stauning, who was prime minister 1924-26 and again 1929-42.

In 1921 the Institute of Theoretical Physics was opened in Copenhagen. It became one of the leading centres in the world for atomic research, and in 1923 its founder, Niels Bohr, received the Nobel Prize. In 1925 Kastrup Airport in Copenhagen was brought into use, and the following year the Danish State Radio was set up.

The Wall Street Crash in 1929 and Britain's subsequent suspension of the gold standard in 1931 meant the collapse of unrestricted capitalism. In 1933 a remarkable political agreement was reached between the Social Democrats and the Liberals, introducing protectionism (to help the farmers) and a number of social reforms (to help the working class), according to which social assistance in case of unemployment, illness, old age, handicaps, etc., became a civil right.

Throughout the 1930s the Social Democratic party obtained about 40% of the votes, but because of the proportional representation, introduced in 1920, it never reached a complete political majority in contrast to Norway and Sweden. No private companies were nationalized, but state control increased, as did the taxes, to secure a more even distribution of wealth.

The reduction of the military, which had been going on since the end of World War I, was stopped in 1934 in view of Hitler's firm establishment of power in Germany. Unemployment was fought by state-backed projects such as construction of roads and bridges, e.g. the Little Belt Bridge between Jutland and Funen, inaugurated in 1935. The standard of housing for the common people improved greatly in the 1930s. The new apartment houses (built of brick) all had running water, central heating, gas and electricity. Many of the flats even included a bath tub and an open balcony. Allotment gardens outside the towns were obtained on easy terms. The standard of public schools was also raised considerably, and an excellent system of public libraries was created. It was no wonder that Th. Stauning was looked upon as a father of the people by the lower classes, but was disliked by those who had to pay for all these social improvements.

The greatest architectual monuments from the interwar period are the Grundtvig Church in Copenhagen, constructed out of six million yellow bricks, a final specimen of the national neo-gothic tradition, and the Town Hall and the University in Aarhus in a far more modern style. This university was the first to be founded in the provinces. Since the turn of the century Aarhus had increasingly assumed the role of Denmark's second city with a population of 125,000 in 1939 although only one eighth the size of Copenhagen. The total population of Denmark was a little over 4 million people.

After Hitler's annexation of Czeschoslovakia Denmark signed a non-aggression pact with Germany in June, 1939. As soon as World War II broke out in Sept. 1939 rationing of certain items such as sugar and coffee was introduced. The winter of 1940 was extremely cold, and ice blocked the Danish ports for a long time, which resulted in a shortage of raw materials, principally fuel.

The general belief in Denmark was that the country would be able to remain neutral as in World War I. But in the early morning of April 9, 1940, most Danes were awakened by low-flying German airplanes. At 4.15 a.m. the German armoured divisions crossed the frontier, and German troops landed in various ports while other strategic points were occupied by air-borne troops. At the same time an ultimatum to stop all resistance was handed to the foreign minister. With German airplanes circling over the king's residence a meeting between the king, the leading members of the government and the military chiefs resulted in a surrender under protest, as there was absolutely no chance of allied support. (Winston Churchill had admitted that the geography of Denmark made it indefensible). The hopelessly unequal confrontations near the frontier were stopped at about 7.00 a.m.

Officially Germany occupied Denmark "to protect it against British aggression". In reality Denmark was only a gateway to Norway, which was important to Germany for two main reasons. The Norwegian fjords were to be bases for the German U-boats, and German control of Norway would secure the entire Swedish export of steel for herself. The fact that the same would be true of Danish exports of farm produce was merely a welcome side-effect.

The Danish acceptance of the German ultimatum meant that the king and the government remained in office, and that the country did not fall under direct German rule. But there was a great fear that the Germans might demand a government led by the Danish Nazi Party, which was a boisterous and much hated group that represented a mere 2% of the voters. On the day after the occupation members of the two big opposition parties stepped into the government to reinforce it. The result of this internal political compromise was that the price index for the wages was abolished, while the prices of farm products grew. So did unemployment, but as industry learned to take up production of substitutes of all kinds, and the old-fashioned digging of peat from the bogs to replace coal was resumed on a grand scale, unemployment decreased somewhat again in 1941.

The dominant question during the "five dark years" of the occupation naturally became whether to choose a policy of adjustment or of confrontation with the occupiers. In the beginning there was no significant opposition to the policy of adjustment. People were paralyzed, and the Nazi power was overwhelming, not least after the collapse of France. But as time went on, and Britain managed to survive, people began to hope again, and everybody began to listen to the Danish news service from the B.B.C. in London.

The most active service for the Allies was carried out by half of the Danish merchant marine that sailed for Britain. A number of Danish ambassadors declared themselves "free". The ambassador in Washington made an agreement with the U.S. government to allow American bases in Greenland, and the Danish governor of the Faroe Islands co-operated with the British occupiers there.

The first flagrant break with legality happened when Germany attacked the Soviet Union in June, 1941, and 269 leading Communists, including members of the parliament, were arrested by the Danish police as an "act of security". This meant that the policy of confrontation gained ground. Illegal news letters began to circulate, and some primitive sabotage actions took place.

Gradually the German pressure on the government increased, and a growing number of unemployed workers were obliged to accept jobs in Germany. In April, 1942, a number of prominent personalities, including the Communist leader as well as the leader of the Conservative Party, founded the first important illegal newspaper. The former was soon captured and later ended up in a German concentration camp, whereas the latter escaped to Britain via Sweden.

In Sept. 1942 King Christian X celebrated his 72nd birthday. Hitler sent him a 165-word-long telegram. The king's brief reply, "Express my best thanks", infuriated Hitler. This "telegram crisis" finally resulted in the resignation of the prime minister, Vilhelm Buhl, who had succeeded Stauning who had died shortly before. The new leader of the government was E. Scavenius, a diplomat who had been the foreign minister during World War I, and whom the Germans considered more pliable.

In March, 1943, the Germans showed their goodwill by allowing a national election to take place. The people voted wholesale for the four old parties, less than 3% voted for the Nazi Party. At the same time a real resistance movement was being organized, the number of acts of sabotage increased, mainly against companies working for the Germans, and against railway lines in Jutland, because they were of great importance for the tranportation of German troops to and from Norway.

In August the Danish sabotage was met by curfews and other German reprisals. In several provincial towns people responded by leaving their jobs and closing their shops. Assaults on German soldiers also took place. A crisis was reached in Copenhagen on August 29, when a saboteur was executed. The Germans declared martial law, including death penalty, prohibition of strikes, etc. The small Danish army was interned, but the naval ships were scuttled just before they were due to be taken over.

On August 30 the government resigned, and the parliament stopped its work. For the rest of the war the country was administered by the leading civil servants. No new government was appointed.

This was a complete victory for the policy of confrontation. After this the Allies gradually began to accept Denmark as an Allied country. On Sept. 16 the leading resistance groups formed "Denmark's Freedom Council", a secret underground government, which soon organized a first-rate communication via Sweden to Britain. An important result was that the Royal Air Force began regular drops of arms and ammunition to the resistance movement.

At this time professor Niels Bohr, who in 1940 had published his theory of atomic fission, secretly left the country to become an adviser at Los Alamos, where the American atomic bomb was being developed.

In September the Germans executed several saboteurs, and on Oct. 2 all those who had one-eighth Jewish blood were to be arrested. However, a high official of the German embassy, G.F. Duckwitz, leaked the plan. The result was that less than 500 of 7,000 Jews were captured. In the following weeks the resistance movement organized the transportation of the remainder on fishing vessels to Sweden. Together with the captured Jews the detained Communists were sent to German concentration camps. They were soon to be followed by a number of people from the resistance movement, as many were caught in the autumn because of information from Danish Nazis.

Now the liquidation of informers began, and this was officially endorsed by the Freedom Council at New Year, 1944. The German answer to this was a brutality, which Denmark had never experienced before. People in the streets were shot at random, and buildings were blown up. The winter of 1944 was the most sinister period of the occupation, but many details of what happened have not yet been revealed as the Danish archives still remain closed – officially to protect those who undertook the liquidations as certain mistakes were inevitable.

In the first months of 1944 there were but few acts of sabotage. The Allied countries were busy building up their own stocks of ammunition, but from May onwards the R.A.F. vastly increased its drops as it was of great importance to disorganize the German military anywhere at the time of the invasion of Normandy on June 6th. Railway sabotage was particularly important. If it could not stop, at least it could delay and confuse the transfer of German troops from Norway to the new front, and these actions saved the Allies from bombing railway installations in Denmark. But the greatest act of sabotage was carried out in Copenhagen on June 22, when the only big plant designed for military industry in Denmark was reduced to a ruin. This resulted in a message of personal thanks from General Eisenhower.

In the following days eight resistance movement people were executed, as well as a number of buildings, including the Concert Hall of the Tivoli and some popular meeting halls, were blown up by a uniformed group of Danish Nazis, the Schalburg Corps, for which reason such acts of counter-sabotage were called "schalburgtage".

In the following week a state of siege was declared in Copenhagen. A "People's Strike" developed followed by demonstrations, riots and casualties. For a time the water, gas and electricity supplies were cut by the Germans. Even when they were reopened, the strike continued until the Schalburg Corps was removed from the city, which was what the Freedom Council had demanded in the form of illegally printed proclamations. After this the Freedom Council obtained diplomatic relationship also with the Soviet Union.

During the "People's Strike" the Danish police offered no help to the Germans, who now looked upon it as a potential danger in case of an invasion. On Sept. 19 in a surprise action all over the country 2,000 out of 9,000 policemen were arrested and transported to German concentration camps. Even then nobody knew how frightful those camps were. But the effect was of course that most of the other policemen went underground and provided the resistance movement with a very important asset: technical skill and inside information about German organizations in Denmark.

The autumn of 1944 and the winter of 1945 saw an increased number of sabotage actions, British bombings of the three Gestapo headquarters in Denmark (called for by the resistance movement) and an influx of ¼ million German refugees from Eastern Germany. To prevent riots and disorder after the liberation which was approaching, talks began between the Freedom Council and the leading politicians.

At the end of April 1945 Hitler committed suicide, and Allied forces reached Hamburg and Lübeck. On May 4, at 8.34 p.m., just when the Danish news bulletin was on the air from the B.B.C. the announcer stopped and said, "We have just received an important message. The Allied Headquarters have announced that the German troops in N.W. Germany, Holland and Denmark have surrendered." Although the official surrender was set for the morning of the next day, people immediately tore down the blackout curtains, put candles in the windows and poured into the streets, rejoicing.

Thus Denmark fortunately escaped from being a battlefield although Liberation Day, May 5, did not pass without casualties. There were still more than 150,000 German military and other persons in Denmark, not counting the refugees, but it was the 2,500 armed Danish Nazis who caused the casualties. The resistance movement, numbering 43,000, took power, and began arresting the latter as well as other German sympathizers. This was also to prevent lynching. From Sweden, where more than 20,000 Danes had sought refuge, a Danish Brigade of 5,000 men, who had received military training there, arrived to reinforce the resistance movement.

During the war warm and friendly feelings had developed between the Danes and the Norwegians. Amidst the rejoicing it was feared that Norway was to be the last fortress of the Nazis, but a few days later the Germans surrendered there also.

But the situation of the Danish island of Bornholm in the Baltic Sea east of the dividing line between the Western powers and the Soviets became serious. The German commander refused to surrender to the Russians with the result that they bombarded its two main towns, Rønne and Nexø, on May 7, and occupied the island on May 9. After almost a year the Russians abandoned the island, and handed it back to Denmark officially on April 5, 1946.

On May 5, 1945, the king, who had been prisoner in his own palace since Sept. 1944, asked the former prime minister, V. Buhl, to form a new government, which came to consist of an equal number of "old" politicians and members of the Freedom Council. A few days later the parliament resumed its functions.

In 1947 king Christian X died at the age of 77, and was succeeded by his eldest son, Frederik IX.

A month after the liberation Denmark was accepted as a member of the United Nations. The government declared that Denmark had no territorial claims on German soil, which was to be a matter of great controversy in the coming years, as South Slesvig had its population doubled by refugees, while the Danish minority, after 12 years of hard suppression, reasserted itself with unexpected force. The idea of redrawing the border line, however, never gained support in the parliament.

The great domestic issue after the liberation was a judicial settlement. Laws with retrospective application for the time of the occupation were introduced, including the death penalty, which was applied in 46 cases. But as there had been no clear lines in the first part of the occupation, the judicial purge was not consistent. Consequently many people from the resistance movement turned away from politics. Others joined the established parties. In the election held in Oct. 1945 the Communists obtained 18 seats in the parliament (out of 150). In 1947 this was halved to nine, and this meant that until 1972 the political stage was again dominated by the four old parties.

The general situation of Denmark after the war was much better than in most of Europe (except for such neutral countries as Sweden and Switzerland). There had been less destruction, and the state of health of the population was good. But the economy was ruined. The German occupation had cost Denmark what was equivalent to 1 ½ year's Gross National Product. Industry was hopelessly antiquated. In the meantime especially American industry had made tremendous steps forward in technology, chemical engineering, etc. Half of the merchant marine was lost, and lack of fuel and other materials meant that rationing was tightened in the early postwar years. For several years the ¼ mill. German refugees were an extra burden to be paid for by increased taxes.

From 1948, however, the situation in Europe eased after the Marshall Aid from the U.S. began, and the Organization for European Economic Cooperation was created.

In the same year the Faroe Islands in the Atlantic Ocean with a population of 40,000 obtained Home Rule, but remained a part of the Danish kingdom.

After the Communist coup d'etat in Czechoslovakia in 1949 Denmark left its traditional policy of neutrality, and joined NATO. Britain devalued the pound by 30%, and Denmark followed, which reflected the new balance of economic power. It caused some inflation, but generally the 1950s developed into a period of economic stability with a growing mechanization of the farming industry, a renewal of industrial plants and fishing vessels while new hotels made way for American tourism. A notable building from the 1950s is the Louisiana Museum of Modern Art north of Copenhagen, paid for by Knud W. Jensen, a business man as well as a well known intellectual. It was at this time that baroness Karen Blixen, who had written "Out of Africa" in 1937, reached international fame as a storyteller.

In 1953 Denmark changed its constitution. Female succession to the throne was made possible, the Upper House of the parliament was abolished, and Greenland (the world's largest island with a population of almost 50,000 people) was no longer to be a colony, but was given the status of a Danish county. A new institution, "The Ombudsmand", was introduced to oversee ministries and other state institutions for possible bureaucratic abuse (this idea was later taken up by other countries).

The effect of the Soviet suppression of Hungary in 1956 was that the Danish Communist Party gradually disappeared from the political stage, and a new party on the left wing, the People's Socialist Party, grew up on its ruins. In 1959 Denmark took part in the creation of the European Free Trade Association (EFTA).

From about 1960 the international boom set in, which was to change the old pattern of society completely. Expanding industry attracted people not least from the farming sector where the number of small farms was tremendously reduced. Foreign workers, principally from Yugoslavia, Turkey and Pakistan, were allowed to take jobs. Television, tape recorders and other new forms of media internationalized not only information, but music, new fashions, etc., to an extent never seen before. The towns expanded rapidly, and as ownership of the private car spread, and new roads and bridges made it possible, industrial plants were placed far away from the old city centres. In the 1960s and 1970s more buildings were constructed in Denmark than in the previous 1000 years. The greatest single project was the new Technical University north of Copenhagen, but the most daring piece of engineering was the construction of the new fishing harbour of Hanstholm on the northwest corner of Jutland, the most wind-swept point of the country. Also the new art museums of Aalborg, Holstebro and Herning, all in Jutland, should be mentioned.

In 1961 the electoral age had been reduced from 23 to 21 years, and the percentage of young people who received a higher education went up from 4 to 30%. A natural consequence of this was the "Rebellion of the Youth" in 1968, which broke up the old authoritarian systems not only within the universities, but in society in general. It became common to address people by the more intimate form of "du" instead of the polite "De" (cf. German du/Sie and French tu/vous).

This was again followed by the "Women's Liberation" beginning around 1970. The growing demand for labour meant that women had to be educated and find jobs as well as men. Rightly they felt that they had been suppressed, but it resulted in a growing number of divorces and a destabilization of the old patriarchal family pattern. Many decided to live in collectives, the most famous of which is "Christiania" in Copenhagen, where some 800 people settled in old disused military buildings.

Under Social Democratic rule Denmark developed into a welfare state and was the first country in the world to create a ministry of environment in 1971. The grassroots organizations obtained unusually strong adherence. They prevented Denmark from building atomic power plants, and laid the basis for a growing production of wind mills for the generation of electricity.

In the beginning of 1972 King Frederik IX died and was succeeded by his oldest daughter, *Margrethe II*, according to the new constitution. This happened just about 600 years after Margrethe I had taken over from her father as the only former female sovereign.

EFTA (the European Free Trade Association) made a great contribution to the good economic times of the 1960s, but much to the detriment of Denmark it never liberalized trade in farm produce, so when our greatest buyer, Britain, approached the EEC, popularly called the European Common Market, Denmark followed. This caused great internal strife because of the much more centralized organization of the EEC than the EFTA.

The right wing parties were much in favour of it, whereas the People's Socialist Party was opposed, and the large Social Democratic Party was split. However, its leader, the prime minister J.O. Krag, put every ounce of his energy into the fight in favour of the entry, cooperating with the biggest private companies. His argument was that Danish farm exports would be ruined if we were left outside the EEC. In a referendum on Oct. 2nd, 1972, in which 90% of the electorate participated, the outcome was 63.5% in favour and 36.5% against. After having announced this result, Krag, who was only 58, resigned the office as prime minister to the great shock of the entire population. He undoubtedly realized that to heal the split of the party a person from the centre of the party was needed.

Until 1972 Denmark had been known for its great political and social stability, but the internal disputes over the EEC question together with the oil crisis and the growth of bureaucracy destabilized the political patterns in the years from 1972 to 1982. Ten or more political parties obtained seats in the parliament. Unemployment, inflation and the national debt began to grow rapidly, while the computer age reached the country.

In 1982 the much reduced Radical Party decided to abandon its traditional support of the Social Democratic rule, and for the first time since 1901 a Conservative leader became prime minister. The result was cuts in the social benefits, a considerable reduction of unemployment, but a continued growth of the national debt.

In 1986 the Common Market countries (Germany, France, Britain, Italy, Holland, Belgium, Luxemburg, Ireland, Greece, Spain, Portugal and Denmark) passed the first amendment act of its constitution, the aim of which was to make way for a political union and to abandon the remaining trade barriers. If it had not been for Denmark, this would have been passed almost unnoticed. This time, however, the Danish Social Democrats stood firm, and declared that Denmark had entered the Common Market on certain conditions, which were not to be changed. The result was that the amendment act had to be exposed to a new referendum in Denmark.

To explain this step, which was highly unpopular among the EEC politicians, it should first be remembered that to ask the people can never be undemocratic. Secondly that Denmark is in a special situation, being the bridgehead between Europe and the other Scandinavian countries, which are not in the EEC. A possible EEC Union does not only involve the Scandinavian passport union, but it is a matter of taxation and social welfare, etc. If all barriers in the EEC were removed, taxation would have to be harmonized, which might endanger the Scandinavian progress in social welfare, environmental precautions, etc. Against these arguments it is maintained that the Danish viewpoints will have a greater effect within the EEC than without. The Scandinavian countries will never be able to influence world politics, whereas a united Europe might add a bit of European scepticism to American foreign policy and be a mediator between East and West.

The referendum was held on Feb. 27, 1986. Only 75% of the electorate took part, and the result was an acceptance of the amendment act of the Common Market by 56% against 44%, which reflected the doubts and hesitations among the Danish people as to the path to the future.

But the ultimate hope of the Danes is no doubt the same as of all other people that we can protect our world against destruction and extend democracy and welfare everywhere.

LIST OF DANISH KINGS

INDEX

INDEX

REFERENCES

References

"A History of Denmark" by Palle Lauring, Høst & Søn, Copenhagen, 1960.

"The Story of Denmark" by Stewart Oakley, Faber & Faber, London, 1972.

"Prehistoric Denmark". The National Museum, Copenhagen, 1978.

"Denmark, An Archaeological Guide" by Elisabeth Munksgaard, Faber & Faber, London, 1970.

"A Danish Gospel. Illustrated with pictures from Danish Churches" by James Mellon, British embassador to Denmark, Centrum, Copenhagen, 1986.

"A Bibliography of Danish Literature in English Translation 1950-80 with a Selection of Books about Denmark" by Carol L. Schroeder, published in 1982 by Det Danske Selskab, The Danish Institute for Information about Denmark, Kultorvet 2, DK-1175 Copenhagen K.